MONASTIC PRINCIPLES

MONASTIC PRINCIPLES

By: Fr. Raphael El-Baramousy

Monastic Principles

ST SHENOUDA MONASTERY
8419 Putty Rd,
Putty, NSW, 2330
Sydney, Australia

www.stshenoudamonastery.org.au

ISBN 13: 978-0-9941910-5-2

Cover Design:

Hani Ghaly
Begoury Graphics
www.Go2printOnline.toprint.com.au

Contents

The Story of This Book

I do not claim that I follow a perfect monastic life nor have I achieved a level of spirituality that allows me to write a book on monastic life, I am still a beginner. It is simply my heart's desire and my soul's longing to live a monastic life in its essence. How do we live this essence in truth and all honesty? And has its meaning changed in the twenty first century compared to previous centuries?

I asked myself one, or indeed, two questions, for which I had no answer. Puzzled, I began to research monastic heritage books, which were left to us by the great fathers of the wilderness who wrote about this angelic life. My research scattered some of the clouds of confusion and I was attracted by the light, so I continued to contemplate and follow it with my eyes wide open and with an eager mind. Then I received the answer to my questions which I have recorded on these pages and thus produced this book.

The purpose of recording these answers in a book is for my fathers and brothers the monks to accompany me in these monastic yearnings, that we may reach the goal for which we have abandoned the whole world and separated ourselves from everyone to unite with the One.

I ask God through the intercessions of our mother, the virgin St. Mary and the prayers of His Holiness Pope Shenouda III, and his partner in the apostolic church our father the Bishop Isizorous the abbot of the Baramous Monastery, that this goal be realised. His Grace Bishop Isizorous is a living book on true monastic life. I thank him from all my heart for his effort, advice and mentorship, may God reward him with heavenly gifts.

Signed,

A monk from Shiheet

Introduction

Our Coptic Orthodox Church understood and lived the bible in its deep spirituality and longed for the life of righteousness since the day she was conceived. From here, monastic life appeared as a model of Christian life which seeks righteousness and the fulfilment of Christ's words: "If you want to be perfect, go, sell what you have and give to the poor and you will have treasure in heaven; and come, follow Me." (Matt 19:21). Thus, monastic life is God's calling to a life of righteousness, a calling that cannot be fought, a current of spiritual desire that cannot be stopped and a pure sacrifice poured on God's altar of love. For none of those who came to monastic life were ever hesitant or shaken, but were filled with the fire of God's love which kindled in their hearts, they cut off all links with the world and cleared all hurdles to reach the heavens, where they were welcomed onto the holy mountains and into God's bosom with kindness and compassion.

Through this understanding, it is feasible to say that a monk is one who maintains the zeal of love kindled in him till death, but rather, fuels it each day increasing its flame, desire and endeavour without ceasing.

Monastic life is biblical in its behaviour, in that it is based on the teachings of the bible and follows its spirit. The bible teaches us to follow Jesus Christ and use Him as the role model. All monastic rules are combined in those two teachings, and a monk organises his life according to them and carries his cross every day. Therefore, a monk, in this world, represents Christ the sufferer and does not see himself other than hanging on the cross, so that his body may not rest on earth. He experiences each day the moments of Good Friday and continuously awaits Easter Sunday with hope.

Monastic life is summarised in the spilling of the soul and the offering of one's life in the hands of Christ, the groom of our souls, that He may become everything for us. We devote every moment of our lives for the glory of His name, our King whom we love. Monks are those whose souls and hearts have dissolved with the love of Christ, abandoned everything even themselves and left the world to come to the wilderness to exchange their worldly love with another. They came to find peace and serenity and to obtain purity of heart and mind to be able to pray a pure prayer in the presence of God that He may become the fulfilment of all their desires, happiness and comfort, and so, they praise God day and night without ceasing.

A monk in his detachment from the world longs for God, for he sees the whole world in the heart of God. He leaves behind all worldly desires and earthly life to fulfil God's will, not his. He treads a path opposing to the current of earthly life: he is content with little, and from the divine gifts he is never content. He is hungry for righteousness and does not live on earthly bread. The world is materialistic, it seeks money and the fulfilment of worldly desires for the sake of an earthly life that will perish, whereas monastic life is spiritual and ascetic for the sake of a life in the kingdom of heaven.

A monk is a living martyr, but without the worldly glory. A martyr that has not been shredded by the teeth of a lion, a martyr of deep divine love, and a martyr of active prayer that performs. A martyr of vigilance, isolation and tears in calling for spiritual love. A martyr of the final hour, who dies daily for God. A monk is one who is prepared to exile every thought for the sake of Christ and is constantly inflamed with the Holy Spirit. He can see visions at night when everyone else lacks basic vision. After a long journey fraught with danger and pain, a monk finds peace with God and in God, in all his days. God walks with the monk on this difficult road, casting His wings over him to enter the door and find refuge in the shadow of the Almighty. The long road overlooks the door, the door of monumental hope. Behind the door is grace, mercy, light and life, unmatched and unimaginable beauty. One hope in this life is to bravely fight, carrying the cross of love that carries in it celebrations of the resurrection that cannot be expressed.

A monk's personality is very unique, in it; Jesus combines traits of contradicting nature. It combines real freedom with complete obedience, humility with authority, absolute purity with sensitive feelings. With these feelings the monk praises God in the fragrance of His flowers, in the bright light of His stars dancing in space, in the sound of birds singing before day break, in the trickling of water between trees. A monk's word is straight, he does not twist or hide behind interpretations, he does not point to one thing and mean another. His thought, speech and actions are in sync. Therefore, he is easy to deal with, he is clear, direct, honest, unequivocal and does not cheat.

Monastic life declares to the whole world the possibility of living a life of purity and righteousness on this earth despite all its worldly temptations. It declares that Christ our Lord can still live in people's hearts, people of this earth, not of another planet. It declares that behind the pains of Good Friday are resurrection celebrations and that behind the dark tomb is the light of eternal life. While we contemplate these thoughts we are ashamed, and ask, has the march been delayed?!! Has faith been extinguished? Is sanctity scarce? Has strong testimony been weakened? Has warm love grown cold?!! We must examine ourselves in order to return to our "first love" and restore Christ's image. It is our responsibility to tread in the path of righteousness in monastic life and it is our duty to once again restore our position as real ambassadors for Christ in this world. Only then, will we deserve to affiliate ourselves to the monastic life that we have loved and chosen to live.

Monastic Principles

Monastic life is essentially an invitation to venture into the deep, as the Lord said: "Launch out into the deep" (Luke 5:4). The soul is this depth which we enter and delve into its deepest corners which our minds have not yet been able to understand or comprehend. Humanity has recruited the best minds and philosophers to explore its depths and understand its essence and until now, even after a long time, they have not been able to discover its secret and have not reached its depths - there lies "one pearl of great price" (Matthew 13:46). This is not strange as the secret is God's and He reveals it to those who fear Him.

A monk carries with him the greatest commandment with utmost importance "You shall love the Lord your God with all your heart, with all your soul, and with all your mind. This is the first and great commandment" (Matthew 22:37). He clutches onto this commandment and follows it closely all his life - this is the essence of monastic life. Monastic practises and traditions are merely an expression of our love to the Lord that burns in our heart. Monastic traditions are not the goal; rather they are the means of maintaining the fire of God's divine love burning within us. God is everything and He is the goal and our focal point. A monk is a person who has loved God and favoured Him above all "He who loves father or mother more than Me is not worthy of Me." (Matt 10:37).

An intimate, loving relationship has been established between Christ and the monk, to the extent that St. Paul says "it is no longer I who live, but Christ lives in me" (Galatians 2:20).

Monasticism is a meaningless way of life if Christ's love is not present in it. Christ's love fills the life of a monk; it is a sacrificial love that penetrates to the depth of the soul and heart. Because this love is continuously growing and renewed, monastic life is not routine and stale, but rather it is dynamic and renewable. It becomes an easy, balanced, sweet and joyful life that springs forth from the perfect and genuine love of Jesus Christ.

The love of God conflicts with the love of the world which involves nothing but "the lust of the flesh, the lust of the eyes, and the pride of life" (1 John 2:16). Thus the essence of monastic life is the removal of worldly love and replacing it with God's love, the latter is noble and greater than the first, and they can never be mixed. Loving Christ is the basis, the bond, the centre point, the crown and the heart of monastic life. The calling of this love is what pushes the monk to leave everything behind. It is important for this love to continue to grow; otherwise the real meaning of monastic life will be ruined. This love is not taught in books and cannot be attained by repetition, it is rather a seed planted by God in the heart of the person and it is for the monk to continue to care and tend to it so that it can grow and yield fruit.

Love That Has Power To Drive

The love of God in a monk's heart is not simply a passing moment or a temporary enthusiasm that dissipates when the hour of agony strikes or when darkness appears. On the contrary, it has the power to ignite a monk's emotions and drives him to persevere. It has the power to drive a monk to maintain his relationship with God regardless of pain and suffering even when the clouds appear dark. It has power which allows a monk to feel indescribable things driving him to do what pleases God.

A monk fixes his sight on loving Christ and steers his path towards Him. He ties his destiny to Him; he is a person who longs to reach the depths. A monk is a person who wants what is better and seeks to delve into the deep. Christ's life was revealed to him with its attractive features, and so he refused to settle for any other love. For the sake of this love, he abandoned everything even freeing himself from all the worldly desires of money, fame and luxuries of life. Having put his hand on the plough and walked the narrow path, he has one goal, and that is to strengthen his love with Christ and to make his life a living declaration that Christ is the only one that deserves our complete love.

Love That Reflects On Others

If a monk's heart is filled with God's love, naturally, it will be filled with love towards his brethren. The words of the bible are clear "By this all will know that you are My disciples, if you have love for one another." (John 13:35). Since monastic life is a relationship of love, it becomes clear why a communal way of life that is established on unconditional love is necessary. The fire of the Holy Spirit in the heart of a monk reflects on others through the unconditional and non-discriminatory love he has towards others. If a monk shows compassion to some and not others, tends to some and ignores others or shows any preferential treatment, then it portrays a lack of real love.

Therefore, Jesus Christ remains the perfect role model of unconditional love for the monk to follow. Monks love everyone, because they love Christ, and they are in Christ. Love is a ladder a monk climbs to reach the heavens to be close to Christ. If a monk has no love, then for what reason does he fast till dusk, and for what reason does he worship till he sweats?!! If a monk is not quick to serve his brothers, then he needs to revise the first point in monasticism, which is love. Love is the alphabet of monasticism. If God's love ruled the heart of a monk, it will make him serve others with complete honesty and submission, just like Jesus Christ. While Jesus is the Master and Lord, He did not shy away from washing the feet of His disciples as He said "If I then, your Lord and Teacher, have washed your feet, you also ought to wash one another's feet." (John 13:14). This kind of love then is generated in the heart of a monk, it is a love mixed with humility, sacrifice and the ability to give without expecting in return.

The Following Of Christ

Following Christ is the goal of every monk's soul and one that consumes their whole life. Following Christ is not only achieved externally, but with the heart and soul as well. We can display Christ's image only after He has reached the depth of our minds, He will then be manifest in our speech and actions just as He is in our minds. This goal must always be in our sight and we must seek it with a strong will. This goal must dictate a monk's life and must be the basis which leads him from place to place.

The essence of monastic life is the continuous discovery of Christ and the aspiration to be like Him and to follow Him regardless of the hurdles we face on the road. The clarity of this goal in our lives will fill our lives with Christ's light and will cause us to continuously aspire to what is better. It will emit confidence in a monk's spirit, which will drive him to desire the source even more and sacrifice himself for it. When we talk about following Christ as being the essence of monastic life, it means that we choose to be poor, virgins, and obedient just like Jesus was.

   Asceticism (poverty by choice):

Jesus Himself was poor "Foxes have holes and birds of the air have nests, but the Son of man has nowhere to lay His head" (Luke 9:58). There are two types of poverty; the one which consists of materialistic and the other consisting of one's self (deprivation of one's honour, dignity i.e. to be a nobody). Materialistic poverty is a means of reaching poverty of one's self; the latter is obvious in St. Paul the apostle's saying "It is no longer I who live, but Christ..." (Galatians 2:20). The poverty of one's self is the foundation of true poverty, as for the external (materialistic) poverty, it is based on perception and can change over the ages. Thus the key is complete deprivation, regardless of how small things might seem.

Virginity And Chastity:

It should be noted that such a lifestyle may seem beyond human nature; however, it is within our reach. We cannot deny that human love and affection were integrated in the creation of humanity; however, there is a love that is stronger and far more superior, love that can not only absorb the human love and surpass it, but is also able to maintain the virginity of the body and soul. A monk challenges the rules of nature, he destroys and overcomes these obstacles so that he can honestly live for the goal for which he has left the world.

Obedience:

What does obedience really mean? Obedience is like poverty, in that it is the deprivation of freedom and will. We have an example to emulate, which is Jesus Christ when He said in His payer "not My will, but Yours, be done" (Luke 22:42). Obedience indeed requires balance, not from the doer only, but also from the requester. Thus Obedience helps the monk discover God's will in his life.

A Cross And A Resurrection

We know that life and death are opposites that do not combine, but in Christ, death was absorbed by life. Jesus Christ to whom is all glory, died on the cross and overcame death with His own death, and so, resurrection came forth from death. In order for us to live, we must first die "unless a grain of wheat falls into the ground and dies, it remains alone; but if it dies, it produces much grain" (John 12:24). A monk dies every day in order to live. When sin enters a person's life, it destroys the human nature, and so the flesh lusts against the spirit and the spirit against the flesh. As for the monk that carries his cross and lives with Christ, Christ will restore the human nature once again. All spiritual perseverance to quench a desire, lustful behaviour, or any unchristian behaviour is death met with resurrection in the spirit, body and soul.

Therefore, the life of a monk consists of offering one's self on the altar of love to die, so that it can live in a glorified form and thus it is the death of the old, and the birth of the new. The Coptic Orthodox Church understood this correct understanding of monasticism and protected it for us till this day. When a person becomes a monk, they are laid on the ground and covered with the altar's curtain, which symbolises a shroud. Funeral proceedings are performed on them to symbolise their death from their previous life and the world. At the end of the proceedings they arise as a new human and are given a new name, a new uniform and they begin a new life.

Evidently then, monastic practices of virginity, asceticism and obedience, are nothing more than an expression and a meaning of this glorious truth - that the offering of one's self as a sacrifice to God in complete obedience till death, is so that He can resurrect it with Him. This sacrifice is complete - absolute - final, because he who dies does so completely and cannot return back. Thus this death is by adoption and so it loses its horrifying nature. The word adoption here is used in the sense that it is by choice, a conscious decision and not by force or pressure. The monk carries this cross by his own will:

• The cross is the yoke, and the yoke is the essence of the monastic path

• The cross is a holy pledge for the monk to be faithful to Christ his whole life

• The cross is the symbol of a personal life with Christ embraced by the monk

• The cross is the secret lived by the monk in isolation or in company

• The cross is a banner and a symbolic prize of the new life

A Holy Life

A monk will aspire to achieve mainly holiness. Holiness is to be like Christ our Lord as much as possible and to gradually shift from a humanistic world that can be seen and felt, to a spiritual and heavenly one. Our Holy God loves the saints and finds comfort in them. Whenever a monk grows closer in His likeness, God bestows upon him blessings that purify, of which the monk becomes extremely fond of. This requires spiritual wisdom and an alert conscience and subordination to God's will throughout the monk's life.

The existence of saints in the long history of monasticism is proof that these statements about holiness are not theoretical, but they are real and practical. This calling to holiness is plausible even though the road is tough. He who desires a saintly life must understand what to do, where to go and what to practice to get there. The main topic of conversation for a monk is holiness, because it is his permanent nutrition and a spring that never drains.

Note:

Now that we have learnt about the essence of monastic life, we must measure our life in light of what was left to us by our saintly Fathers the hermits and from their monastic heritage and tradition that reveals to us this essence. God has given us minds to think and comprehend, sensitive hearts that can feel, desire, and love. He has given us the free will to direct and take control of our lives. It is then appropriate to say that we have chosen monastic life deliberately based on our heart's desire and love and with our complete free will.

The Cell And Its Spiritual Meaning

Monastery life is the suitable surrounding for a monk to practice ascetic life with his brothers, and to acquire the true monastic spirit. The monastery is a secured fortress and a protective enclosure for the monastic life, in which the community life forms the steps leading towards a holy and righteous life. As for the cell, it is like a dwelling where the groom is alone with his bride. It is a fertile place for the human soul to meet with its heavenly groom. The cell creates for a monk, the quiet and calm environment for a life of contemplation. Within the silent walls of the cell a monk prepares himself for the eternal retreat.

Without the cell, a monk would feel somewhat incomplete. The cell is an inherent part of monasticism, a monk that runs away from it, will be at loss. The cell is the peak of both prayer and effort to purify the soul. Life in the cell is natural for those who practise deep love and tread the path of purity and fix their sight towards the Kingdom. The cell is a suitable place for private perseverance and a place of victory, which appears in its glory among those who insist on fighting the evil hidden within them. Only in the cell the decision is taken to be victorious on all evil wherever it may be.

The cell is seriousness in everything, there is no place for fun and relaxation: it is a place of intimate love between two hearts that cannot be separated, a passionate meeting between an ascetic heart searching for a heart that provides everything. How many monks have seriously treaded towards the cell to find their love, and God was near him, talking and whispering in his ear? He bestows on him from His spirit and performs miracles for him. God cares and supports him in fighting his enemies. He feeds him heavenly food and provides him with water out of stone. God guides him day and night, coaches and teaches him. God enters into a covenant with him. If the days in the cell become long, it is so that the lover submits himself in the hands of his love completely just like the people of Israel submitted into the hands of the Lord in the desert of Sinai. In return, the Lord provides for the monk everything his soul requires to exit the slavery of the devil and enter the freedom and glory of the children of God - just as He did in the past. Thus God then reveals to the monk Himself and His glory.

In the cell, a monk discovers his weaknesses and admits his inability. He realizes how insignificant he is compared to God's incomprehensible love. Everything in the cell invites the monk to contemplate his situation in front of God, who is the only One that occupies his mind, heart, feelings – indeed his whole being. In the cell the monk is faced with either this reality that attracts him, or endless boredom. In this contention, there is no room for the smallest of distractions, time wasting, relaxation or submission. In the cell, it is a continuous quest, continuous perseverance and effort; it is an active life and anticipation of time.

Being in the cell is like traveling from the outside to the inside, from the materialistic world to the mystical world of spirituality, from dwelling with others to the innards of one's soul, from prayer to contemplation, from tangible matters to the battle of desires. Every time this battle is halted, it signifies a retreat from the path of righteousness and this delay leads to deadly despair. Even though this perseverance is tiring for a monk, he cannot stop for a single moment. Depression is lethal, sadness is deadly, distraction leads to delays and amusement is temptation by the devil. The devil of weariness is always lurking behind the door and under the window; waiting for the monk to change his path. The devil does not back away from his goal, because life in the cell is a continuous miracle. In the cell, sin is naked and the extent of its evil is made clear. Therefore repentance from sin has to be with sorrowful weeping. Whenever the monk walks in the corners of his soul, he finds in its depth something else to stir him and the more he scrutinizes himself, the more he will be found hanging his head in shame.

In the cell, a monk practices spiritual practices continuously and contends with the devil in his home and sieges him in every corner. In the heart of the cell is a silent lover pleading with the almighty God of the entire universe with no one to disturb him. The stars alone watch him, only the sun shines upon him through the window, only the sweet breath of dawn touches what is left of his body from skin and bone; it refreshes him in his pleading. He disappears from the eyes of the people to see God within him.

The monk living in the cell may seem simple, naive, not knowing how to compliment or socialize with others and may seem too shy to look others in the eye. He may be dismissed because of his quietness, weakness and low voice. If he made himself known to others, he would be made fun of him for his naivety and he would act even more naive so that others would make fun of him even more.

The cell for the monk is his permanent cross. In it he abandons everything completely and cries continually as Christ did saying "my God, my God, why have you forsaken me" (Psalm 22:1). God looks upon him from above, lifts him up and says "for the Lord your God is with you wherever you go" (Joshua 1:9). Look to your perseverance and pay attention to the tears of your heart. The temptations of the cell are countless: anxiety, doubt, weariness, trouble, solitude and foreignness. This is all because the Lord is absent from it, and the Lord is absent from it to test the extent of a monk's love to Him. He is absent so that the monk would realize that his perseverance is meaningless without the presence of God. Sometimes in the cell, God would abandon His beloved till his eagerness for God's love increases. It is pitiable to be seen as loose and lazy, because that would cause God to remain absent and will leave the monk to fight, stumble, labour and cry out on his own. This is all to prime him to face God and receive God's grace that only those who persevere receive. God will not appear in front of a monk until everything has fallen, and where else would it fall except in the cell!!

A monk in the cell is under cover and unknown. He chooses this to ease the discovery of spiritual matters. He knows that if he craves learning God's secret, he has to be under cover and unknown. When a storm hits, all the trees with roots covered under the ground can stand against the storm. The cell is that inner vigilance, it is the monk's watchfulness, it is like the furnace of fire of the three young men. It combines the fire of continuous spiritual perseverance and the comforting mist of the Holy Spirit.

When a monk enters the cell, he enters his heart. The secret of the existence of a monk is not visible to the human eye, but only inside his heart. This means that any monk that has not yet entered or tried to enter his cell, thus also his heart, has not yet begun his monastic life.

If a monk left the communion of his brothers and entered his cell with laziness and a distracted mind or if he separated from his brothers and became isolated without taking God with him, he will end up without God, his brothers and even himself. This is not the cell, it is something completely different.

The cell is a place that we should fill with our spiritual warmth so that it may become a green pasture for our monastic life and union with God. It is a place to see God in the heart. The cell is a fortress for the strong. It is not an escape, but it is to distance the monk so that he can actively discover, discipline and accustom himself. Only then can he discover God's will in his life.

How marvellous is the cell, in it I see the face of my beloved.

Finally, one of the saints advises us saying:

> Sit in the cell and it will teach you everything
> (Abba Moses the great)

Perseverance In The Life Of A Monk

During the ordination prayers performed on a new monk, a passage from the book of Jesus the son of Sirach is read out which says "Son, when you come to the service of God, stand in justice and in fear, and prepare your soul for temptation." (The Book of Sirach 2:1). This is so that the monk would prepare himself for spiritual battles, of which are the toughest and most violent kind of battles. There are two opposing forces that move a monk: the first pushes him upwards towards the kingdom of heaven, and the second pulls him downwards to earth and pushes him towards the desires of the flesh. There are other battles such as the battles of the thought, actions and speech. When a monk prepares to resist battles against his actions, the battles transfer to his speech and when he has gained control over his speech the battles transfer to his thoughts, which in reality is the toughest kind of battle that requires a high degree of vigilance and watchfulness.

Monastic life requires purity of thoughts, actions and speech. Christ requires us to be righteous, hence, we are striving to continuously persevere spiritually. Thus a monk dusts himself off of any stagnation and arms himself with the grace of the Holy Spirit. The first thing the enemy attacks is the will. Therefore, it is not enough to have the intent to persevere, but actions also are needed. How do we reach the goal? Would we reach it if we were asleep?! Of course not! The kingdom of God is not rewarded to the lazy. Men of strength and war move forward to offer themself as a sacrifice on the altar of love. Only these are rewarded in the kingdom of God. There is no place for those who value their soft skin.

The war is a heated clash to the point where one's will increases and the spirit rises above the body. A monk with a strong will is not afraid to break in through these battles with no regard for himself. The Holy Spirit provides him with limitless power and courage in these battles and leads him from victory to victory. A character of perseverance does not holdup the battle or run from it. Those who have truly placed themselves in the hands of God are certain of their victory in Him and by Him. Uncertainty is not acceptable, because it wastes energy and weakens the will. The battle requires a bold and decisive personality dressed with the Holy Spirit. Decision making for the uncertain is difficult; they are thrown by the waves and go where the wind blows. A spiritual decision to defend in a battle is a heroic act as a result of a mind enlightened by the Holy Spirit. As our spirit opens up to the Holy Spirit and the Holy Spirit dwells within us and supports us in our perseverance, it will extinguish the fire of Satan's arrows. For the rain does not dwell in rocks, but in good soil. Therefore, a monk's perseverance depends on two things: acts of grace in the monk's heart and continuous perseverance without weariness.

A Monk's Role In Spiritual Perseverance

The golden rule in this matter is how honest a monk is in facing spiritual battles and how much the power of God acts in him. As a consequence of losing our honesty in the confrontation, we lose the ability to be with God and the power of God will be withdrawn from us. We then face defeat at the hands of our enemy, Satan, and will stumble over our mistakes. If a monk has a good conscience, it would rebuke him over the smallest lapse, but if he cried out to God and persevered, God is quick to his rescue.

Dishonesty in monastic life consists of:

- Greed and luxury

- Dishonesty in the purity of the body and spirit

- Arrogance

- Laziness and weariness that gives our desires the chance to destroy our effort

- Avarice of the mouth and stomach that fuels wars of impurity

- Seeking comfort from others and not from God

- Wasting time in gossip and useless conversations

Dishonesty in monastic behavior is a breach of the treaty we entered with God and the theft of what we offered on His holy altar when we offered our life i.e. withdrawing what we had offered God (spirit, body and soul). The dishonesty of a monk in revealing his secrets and inner thoughts to his spiritual father prevents God from dwelling in his heart; as a consequence, the monk will continue to suffer from drought in life and the loss of communion with God. Therefore, there is no alternative but to apply pressure on one's spirit till it confesses all its sins and weaknesses in all honesty.

The Role Of The Holy Spirit

The most dangerous thing is the reliance of a monk on himself, without God's support in facing spiritual wars. It is best for this monk that God completely withdraws His support so that he would lose the battles waged against him by the enemy that he may realize that his life is without support. A monk can never succeed unless God Himself is in his heart. Continuous victory in spiritual battles means that God's power and joy is continuously in our minds and hearts. This justifies the need to search the ins and outs of the soul and everything that moves in its depth, so that we do not give our enemy the chance to plant weeds within us and God would then abandon us. We must seek to find the reason for our fall so that we can rise again and return to Him.

The bible always motivates us to pray continuously for one thing and that is to live every moment in the presence of God and His power "Watch and pray, lest you enter into temptation." (Mathew 26:41). God does not gain anything from our prayers, but wants us to pray so that He can provide us with power, peace and victory. There is no protection for the monk from the temptations of the enemy without a continuous and passionate prayer in the heart, which is the flame that burns the desires of the body. Therefore, the secret to continuous victory is in our grasp, because the Lord invites us to Him "I am with you always, even to the end of the age" (Matthew 28:20). A real monk creates a pure prayer in his heart and prepares his conscience to dig within him for weaknesses and desires so that he can chain it and rob its power. Through prayer, a monk enters the depth of his soul, and the further he reaches, the more he cries; I am dust and ashes - I am a worm not a human. A monk concludes that he is not capable of facing the easiest of battles on his own and that relying on himself is vanity of vanities, and so he cries out again and earnestly prays till God's help arrives and strengthens him, then, the circle becomes complete.

The Holy Spirit within us is ready to undertake its active role in facing spiritual battles, if our intention is good, pure, spiritual and for the love of God from all the heart. Christ is relentless in pointing out the original motivation for monastic life, and that is to love God from all the heart. From here, the Holy Spirit begins its work; it supplies the body with the power of patience, the spirit with the power of sacrifice and the will with the power of determination. It really does seem like an abnormal power.

It is impossible for any vigilant monk to say that his perseverance is the secret to his victory. For will and determination are in reality under the control of the Holy Spirit, and so, perseverance becomes mixed with a supreme Godly element. The Holy Spirit can lift spiritual perseverance from the works of humanity to become the works of God, from a level of mind and logic to a miraculous level. Spiritual perseverance where the light and grace of the Holy Spirit has not shone is incomplete and leads to deviation from true monastic life. This is very clear in Abba Anthony's letters concerning the Holy Spirit.

The Holy Spirit is the secret key to spiritual perseverance. If the heart simply requests the love of God, and this love overtakes the spirit and thoughts and controls the will, the monk enters under the guidance of the Holy Spirit to work and persevere wisely with determination that exceeds his own will and determination. The spiritual perseverance lived by the monk does two main things: one from the perspective of the monk and the other from God's perspective. As for the effort required from the monk, it is to push himself by fasting, praying, vigilance and prostrations, fulfilling his strong and complete love for God. As for the work performed by God, it is providing the power of the Holy Spirit to complete the monk's effort for the kingdom and the glory of God.

If a monk relied on himself and excluded the Holy Spirit from his perseverance, he will bloat himself with self-glory or will become tired very quickly, and both are dangerous.

Active Faith In God

One of the essential elements to the success of a monk in spiritual wars is for his faith to be alive. Faith and prayer go hand in hand as in, when faith increases, prayer increases, and whenever prayer increases, faith increases. Prayer is the thermometer of faith, it is not by how much or how often, but by intensity, truthfulness and honor. Therefore, we need to pray in faith. God is in front of us and on our right hand side all the time watching from above aware of everything and watches our perseverance. Therefore, be careful not to let your faith weaken, because, weak faith is revealed by weak prayer and is the result of spiritual decline, which is represented in:

- The indulgence of a monk's feelings in worldly matters, like entertainment and inappropriate laughter.

- Chatting in unnecessary topics with no relation to spiritual life.

- The engagement in gossiping either by talking or listening and the judgment of others.

- Anger, whining, scrutiny, without the fear of God.

- Avoiding prayer so as to avoid facing the truth about one's self.

A monk will then have no remaining power or courage to appear in front of God, and will not enjoy the father-son relationship. All this is caused by weak prayer and the episode is completed by weakened faith and so on.

A real monk has an active faith in God, certain of the promises of God, certain that he can see them, even though they are invisible, certain he has obtained them, even though they have not arrived, certain and pleased with them, even though he has not touched them with his hand. For trust in God must be absolute. We have absolute trust in God that Christ is truthful and able to give and fulfill His promises. If a monk is faced with temptations and battles, he has to put his trust in Christ and persevere in prayer, tears, prostrations, fasting and vigilance, trusting that victory will inevitably come from Him.

A true monk is a martyr 24 hours a day. If he slept, his enemies are prepared to attack him, for the devil does not sleep. A monk can get distracted and sleep, and in his distraction he is attracted by impure thoughts. As we kick the devil and his dirty deeds out of the door, he creeps in through the windows, holes and cracks. Evil powers are innovative in their ways to invade our spiritual vigilance, but in the midst of all this, we trust and believe that God is almighty, the Pantocrator, and so, we cry out in joy "we are more than conquerors through Him who loved us" (Romans 8:37). In all this, "thanks be to God, who gives us the victory through our Lord Jesus Christ" (1Corinthians 15:57).

Traps Set By The Enemy

Just as a monk fixes his sight on the path of righteousness and begins to taste the sweetness and comfort of practicing virtues, Satan begins to set many traps of different types to maximise his chance of catching a prey. The first trap Satan sets is the trap of despair, where the devil draws the picture to the monk of the pain of the body, the long road of asceticism, the monstrosity of his sins and the difficulty of perseverance. If a monk discovered this trap and avoided it, Satan sets another trap completely opposite to the first trap and that is the trap of self-righteousness, where the devil reminds the monk with the weaknesses of other monks so that the monk would compare them to his righteous deeds. If a monk discovers this trap, Satan sets another that compliments the previous trap, which is excessive asceticism, where the devil surrounds a monk with all sorts of compliments, which drives the monk to perform ascetic practices beyond his means. If a monk succeeded in uncovering this trap, Satan will plant in him defiled desires and images fabricated from imagination. As a result, if a monk felt weak and scared, and began to doubt his ability to remain pure, Satan will return to set a trap of doubt in the forgiveness of God to try and put the monk in a state of despair and remind his soul again with the longevity of time, the unbearable difficulty of practicing virtues and the weakness of the body.

If a monk became alert and did not grow weary of his perseverance and remained defiant in the face of these battles, God will comfort and empower him and will assist him in a way he would have never imagined. In these moments, God saves the honest soul that does not surrender its weapons. From here, the importance of daily repentance in front of God becomes clear. The purpose of it is the submission of the soul to the will of God, so that God would reveal to him Satan's tricks and traps, to strengthen his will, because he knows and can feel the presence of God with him in these battles. This also reveals the importance of including the confession father in all aspects of ascetic practices, be it fasting, prayer, vigilance, prostrations, etc. so that these practices can be trained wisely, so that it does not become excessive and alienated (which is one of the battles waged by Satan especially against the inexperienced). Spiritual mentor-ship requires absolute obedience from the disciple for as long as he is under the guidance of his mentor whom he has chosen.

Also, one of the important things that help us become defiant in the face of Satan's tricks and traps is the sacrament of the Holy Eucharist, as we have been resurrected and become victorious through Christ's resurrection. The sacrament of the Holy Eucharist represents Christ our Lord who has risen from the tomb, and He is capable of mending our fractures and treating our wounds, which were inflected by our enemy. The sacrament of the Holy Eucharist gives us growth and nourishes the life within us, it is the pinnacle of unity between a monk and Christ. As such, one of our saintly fathers said: the partaking of a monk in Christ's Holy

Body and Blood causes an explosion of spiritual springs in the life of the monk. By partaking in this Godly sacrifice, it fully integrates our sacrifice with the sacrifice of our saviour. It transforms the emotions, thoughts and actions of the monk to a live sacrifice that does not know the way to drought or death.

The great fathers of the desert have advised us to contemplate in the lives of the saints who reached righteousness and to follow their lead. This is to encourage us in our spiritual perseverance. By contemplating in the lives of saints, we see spiritual principles and virtues in practice and to believe and be comforted that virtues are not theory, but are tangible reality and to believe that even though the path to righteousness is not easy, it is possible. When we read about how they persevered to reach righteousness, it ignites our love for a life of righteousness and eases the burdens of perseverance and teaches us to persevere without boredom or weariness, because the heart is always with God.

Pain And Suffering In The Life Of A Monk

One of the fathers said: a ship would never be destroyed nor would it sink from being hit by storms and raging waves if its captain is an experienced sailor. Likewise, regardless of how often a monk is faced with temptations and suffering of different kinds, his spirit will never be broken as long as he places his life's ship in the almighty hands of God and is guided by the light of His Gospel. Sometimes God sends pain and woes our way and allows it to persist as a way of aiding our spiritual progression. It is necessary for a monk to remain vigilant and to question where he stands in the face of these woes. He must realise and understand the deep meaning and spiritual benefit behind these woes, and he must pray for the ability to withstand these troubles.

This suffering can be deep, but it must be accepted as a way of purification, and this creates hope within us. Pain can protect us from drifting towards impurity and it can help us learn about ourselves from the way it affects us and how we respond to it. The bearing of pain and suffering will open a window to God's grace and so, we must gratefully accept it so that God's love may further grow and deepen within us. We must not think that pain and suffering means that God does not love us and that He sent them as punishment "for whom the Lord loves He chastens" (Hebrew 12:6). Likewise, God disciplines the righteous, so that he may live a better life in the future and realise God's past actions "My brethren, count it all joy when you fall into various trials, knowing that the testing of your faith produces patience. But let patience have its perfect work, that you may be perfect and complete, lacking nothing." (James 1:2-4).

A monk, through experiencing this pain and grief gains a lot of benefits. The earth does not produce unless farmers work tirelessly to prepare it. Humility is one of those benefits and this is what saint Paul the apostle said to us "and lest I should be exalted above measure by the abundance of the revelations, a thorn in the flesh was given to me" (2 Corinthians 12:7). He then arrives at the conclusion saying "And He said to me, My grace is sufficient for you for My strength is made perfect in weakness" (2 Corinthians 12:9). A doctor may treat a patient by cutting open their wound or even completely removing the cause if necessary and so does God the true physician of our bodies and souls. As our Father, He wishes to treat and heal our souls. Remember that what we suffer in the present is easy and light, so let us bear it, because "God is faithful, who will not allow you to be tempted beyond what you are able, but with the temptation will also make the way of escape, that you may be able to bear it" (1 Corinthians 10:13). Remember also, that in this life, God wishes to discipline us, because we are His beloved children, so that in the next life our spirit will be in a state of purity "The Lord has chastened me severely, but He has not given me over to death" (Psalms 118:18).

If a monk gratefully accepts the pain and suffering inflicted on him, then God's love will flood his heart with joy. We must not forget that our Lord Jesus Christ did not come to show us the easy way of life or how to enter through the wide doorway, but to teach us to carry the cross and walk the path of Golgotha, so that we are finally victorious through the resurrection. Pain and suffering will exhaust the patience of a monk and he will fall in the merciless hands of despair, unless he maintains his peace, place his timings in the hands of God and considers the pain he suffers as sharing the suffering of Christ. Bearing the pain draws similarity in the monk to the One who was hanged on a tree. We do not become Christ's disciples by name, but through pain. A real monk who lives in a deep and loving relationship with Christ and in Christ, even when he is in the midst of a furnace of pain feels and experiences deep comfort. The joy of Christ does not abandon his heart, he feels comforted while he moans from the burden of the cross.

Only God can give joy and comfort

Spiritual Growth In The Monastic Life

Monastic life in its essence is a life of repentance, a continual change from within. Its sole purpose is to be united with God. To achieve this goal, it will require a monk's whole life, till his last breath. The most dangerous thought that threatens a monk's life is to think that he has achieved a state of righteousness. The best phrase to encapsulate a monk's daily life is the saying of our teacher St Paul the apostle, "forgetting those things which are behind and reaching forward to those things which are ahead" (Philippians 3:13). Thus it is a life of moving forward that does not stop.

For the monk, God is the only thing he does not get enough of; therefore we hunger and thirst for God not just every day and every moment, but every heart beat. God Himself placed this desire in the depth of the human, so that he would always seek Him. Every worldly desire when exhausted is finished because it is limited, but the desire for God is limitless. When we talk about spiritual growth in monastic life we do not mean perfection of virtues, because virtue is not the goal of monasticism, it is rather the natural fruit enjoyed by the monk as a result of his companionship with God. Virtue comes during forward progression. Intentional growth is the growth in the love of God and the endless satisfaction with Him until the monk reaches unity with God in body, spirit and soul. It is a continuous effort from within, therefore, a monk must not wait for or expect to be rewarded for his perseverance until the last breath. Growth is to be attached to God and to be rooted in Him. From one front we dwell in Him and are attracted to Him and from the other, we are living in Him and are directed towards Him. Monastic life is active and every action leads to growth, meaning that a monk's image changes gradually until it resembles that of Christ in speech, actions and thought "let this mind be in you which was also in Christ Jesus" (Philippians 2:5). This means that everything that is for Christ is for us until His radiant image is imprinted deep within us.

How To Achieve This Growth

Monastic life is a path we tread while carrying with us

and within us God's life. God's life within us empowers us to tread this path forever. A monk's life is made up of two converging realities: the first is that God grants us His power, His light and His grace without limit, because God is within us. This is a fundamental reality that must be entrenched within us, because God gave Himself for us. This warrants us to offer ourselves to God and become His own and this is the second reality. Therefore a life of growth is to open up to God who is within us. There are, however, matters to be taken into consideration lest our efforts are wasted:

(1) Growth Must Be Gradual

A real monk is one who protects the fire of the divine love kindled in his heart till his death. He fuels this flame of love by a continuous flame of enthusiasm over enthusiasm, jealousy over jealousy and desire over desire. This life includes different stages of growth which must be studied well because many fail to grow in their monastic life because they cannot differentiate between the beginning of the road, the middle of it or the end of it. A monk may be harsh on himself in his ascetic practices such as fasting, vigilance, prostration, etc. during the early stages of his monastic life so that he can quickly grow from within, but sometimes that will have the opposite effect. The monk will then begin to wear away bit by bit or feel exhausted and reduce his activity. He may even convince himself that he is in the beginning of the road and feels compassion towards himself, which then gives him a weak start that develops into a habit that continues with him.

The lack of awareness of the gradual progression of spiritual growth drags us into spiritual problems and temptations that we can do without, such as despair, doubt, arrogance, false praise etc. This brings the focus again on the role of the confession father in these sensitive matters that require a vast amount of experience and balance. Trees do not give fruit immediately after plantation but require constant care so that it grows bit by bit till it bears fruit.

(2) Perseverance And Struggle

Perseverance is an indicator that informs us whether monastic life is on the right path, having a struggle full of joy and victory and the glory that awaits us. A monk's struggle to reach righteousness, which is seeing God, reminds him of the road ahead of him and so, he must not stop as the psalmist says "your face, Lord, I will seek" (Psalms 27:8). He vows his inner life everyday as if he is a beginner, but he perseveres continuously to begin. In the lack of struggle often lies the desire to reach the end of our perseverance before God's decision, as well as the desire for tangible growth. If we are not careful we run the risk of temptation to stop our walk. It is not for us to decide timings, it is sufficient that the hand of God supports our perseverance, it is sufficient to be in the hands of God. Regardless of how slow our growth was or how troublesome the kingdom of darkness was, the fact that we progress in our companionship with God, we know that we will make it.

Perseverance against the body and the devil is constant, it is a battle that is seen and unseen at the same time. Spiritual growth occurs through this perseverance. Every time we face difficulties and tribulations and continue to persevere without surrendering, we successfully get through it and grow even further. Therefore, we must not give up or surrender regardless of how much power the devil has gathered against us. We must not fear or tremble knowing that this will work in our favour towards our growth and confirmation.

(3) Confession Father

The confession father ensures a monk's boldness and that he continues to tread the path. We do not grow spiritually by surrendering ourselves to chance, but we are guided by the experience of our fathers, as in by the Holy Spirit who enlightens them and speaks through them. The spiritual father is held accountable in the eyes of God for his children to grow spiritually. Therefore, obeying our confession father secures our growth towards righteousness and protects us from stumbling on the road and pushes us forward beyond the last losses. The relationship between the father and his son is a relationship of love and complete trust from both parties. The confession father must know his children as thoroughly and deeply as possible: their personality, interests, feelings weaknesses, gifts, etc. He loves each one of them as they are for the sake of Christ's love for them, because he is a father in Christ.

(4) Complete Submission To God

Spiritual growth is a joint effort between God and the monk. It is a joint effort between heavenly grace and spiritual perseverance. This is vital because we cannot achieve anything on our own (John 15:5). God is the first factor within us for He provides love and initiative and we respond to His calling. If we turn our hearts away from God, then it is no longer a co-operation. It must then be a balance between God's grace and ones' perseverance, but it's all because of God's graciousness. We must persevere tirelessly (as if our lives depend on it), knowing that without God's grace, protection and initiative it would not be possible.

The road is long and narrow as described by Christ our Lord. It is not appropriate for us to tread this path alone as we will experience fear and uncertainty. What we need is complete submission to God; complete faith in God's perseverance alongside us as He helps us to grow. Our spiritual growth is God's responsibility if we put our faith in Him and devote our tears, vigilance, prayers, fasting etc. Complete submission means it is no longer our will or desire, but we must always be obedient to God's voice. Therefore it is imperative that we:

- Tie our will to our obedience to Christ so that we do not do anything from our own will.

- Do not concentrate on thoughts of success or failure, but think about continuing our perseverance honestly.

- Trust that Christ has taken care of our necessities along the way and persevere, relying on His assistance

- Abandon our humanly wisdom and rely on Christ when facing our enemies.

- The more we submit our will in subordination the more we will feel God work His care and management.

- Regardless of our weakness, Christ will remember our perseverance. In His hand is the crown of eternal life.

In the following pages we will talk about some of the areas of spiritual growth in the life of a monk - obtaining purity of the heart, growth in the life of subordination, growth in the life of prayer, growth in the word of God and growth in asceticism and deprivation.

Obtaining Purity Of The Heart:

In the path of monastic life, the monk goes through phases and levels of purity of the heart. This purity is obtained through constant perseverance and battles of spiritual wars in all its types. The first crown a monk receives is the purity of the heart which must be a constant wish and a daily desire. Purity of the heart is the freedom from the slavery of worldly desire that ruins our lives. It frees our mind and body from all inclinations that lead to sin. Purity of the heart is a new state for the heart; it is a new heart that lives a new life in Christ and by Christ "Create in me a clean heart, O God." (Psalm 51:10).

Whoever desires purity of the heart must veer from all evil to good with the same passion, joy and intention that was applied to evil instead of good.

How To Obtain It:

A life of purity begins from the inside from within the conscience of the monk, so that it may fill his life "Blessed are the pure in heart, for they shall see God." (Matt 5:8). Purity of the heart is a treasure and is the source of all purity; purity of the mind, of the intention, of the senses and body. Purity also comes forth from the body and soul. A pure body is one whose senses has been preserved from the impurity of worldly desires. A pure soul is a soul that has been preserved from the desire that prefers the world and all that is in it. If the purity of the body is threatened by impurity, the purity of the soul is threatened by the lack of affection with God.

The purity of the body is damaged by sexual sin. The purity of the soul is broken by departing away from God, for the departure of the soul away from God kindles all sorts of desires; by sight, by heart and other senses. Therefore it is important for the monk to desire purity of the heart and request it from God and seek it with all his conscience and direct his will to tread in this path regardless of the effort and fight off impurity in all its forms. Purity if adapted willingly and intentionally, and if the monk preserved his body and soul for God, will allow the monk to be in line to receive the Holy Spirit which will increase his purity and chastity. God requires us to be pure so that He can live in us and unite with us. The monk's role is to offer his body and soul as a daily sacrifice to God with love.

Every thought is to be seized for the obedience of Christ, not worldly desires. The soul and the body are to be crucified with all its members on the cross of love, it is sacrificed on the altar of the heart, "those who are Christ's have crucified the flesh with its passions and desires" (Galatians 5:24). The cross means pain, suffering and travail to the point of death yet it is a source of light, sweetness and has power and joy. The pain of the cross is fire that burns anything that threatens the purity of the body and soul, but if the monk starts showing compassion towards his body and fears suffering he will miss out on the chance to offer his sacrifice which is very valuable in the sight of God.

It is then required that the body be controlled, its parts crucified and desires silenced. We need vigilance and perseverance blended with sweat, blood, tears and the comfort of Christ's Holy body and precious blood so that His sacrifice can be united with ours. A monk also requires a vigilant conscience and to light his lamp with the gospel. He is required to stand and scrutinise every move made by the heart, thought and body. He is required to quench any remaining bodily emotions from his heart which control his actions and causes pitfalls. A monk requires a bridle in order to control his thoughts, desires and emotions which will lead him to new paths opening for his thoughts and his will to align with the spirit and its needs. It is a battle between the old and the new within the mind, heart, body and soul with all its inner operations. This battle leads to the victory; it beautifies the attractiveness of a monk to God's love. He who has God's love kindled within him, has endless purity kindled within him, where all forms of sins and its persistence escapes. It does not dare return to him even from far.

The Power Of God

A life of purity is a journey a monk undertakes. He does not end his perseverance to achieve it until the grave. It does not stop at a certain number of years, but it is a perseverance that requires his whole life. God pours grace and power in the heart of the monk to grant him victory as He promised "as I was with Moses, so I will be with you. I will not leave you nor forsake you" (Joshua 1:5). God gives power to the weak; He strengthens the shaking knees, He empowers the weak will and completes the incomplete. This power acts in the monk that performs what he has been compelled with from the perspective of his purity: "If your hand or foot causes you to sin, cut it off and cast it from you.......If your eye causes you to sin, pluck it out and cast it from you" (Matthew 18:8-9), "I discipline my body and bring it into subjection" (1 Corinthians 9:27), "put to death your members which are on the earth" (Colossians 3:5). The work is completed when the monk has persevered to obtain purity, with all his power and will, with the support of the power of God that works behind the scenes in the heart.

Before God asks us to control our body and suppress its members and desires, He secures the path with His power inside us and with us. If we persevered legally to obtain purity, we would obtain a spiritual power within us with which we can grow, suffer and be empowered. A monk's natural abilities (such as will, desire, tolerance and patience) are not adequate with the requirements of a life of purity but God's secret power works alongside the monk's perseverance and this is the undisputed secret to continuous victory. We can then truly understand our Lord's saying "For My yoke is easy and my burden is light" (Matthew 11:30).

A monk's loathing of urges and desires becomes a natural instinct and sin does not find a place to rest within him. Lest anyone misunderstand, this does not mean that urges are completely cut off from the monk, rather, they remain and a monk is vulnerable to them if he becomes lazy, weary or negligent. It must always be in the forefront of our minds that whoever God grants purity of heart is not immune from failure, but he remains in a state where it is possible for him to fall "Therefore let him who thinks he stands take heed lest he fall" (1 Corinthians 10:12), "....all who were slain by her were strong" (Proverbs 7:26). For as long as we are living on earth, we are vulnerable to falling.

A final word on this topic: Words cannot describe the peace and tranquility that rules the life of the monk who grows in a life of purity. This peace and tranquility accompanies the life of purity and this life is rooted further and further.

Growth In The Life Of Humility

Our saintly fathers, who bravely persevered in the desert, spoke often about humility and its importance in the spiritual growth of the monk and the perseverance against false glory and pride. Saint John El-Dargy and Saint Gregory the theologian considered pride to be the child of false glory and it caused the fall of Satan and his angels. Adam and Eve fell in it too and fell from real glory. The temptation of pride requires a long battle and can only be remedied by humility.

Real humility is the overwhelming feeling of the glory of God met with the realization of the weakness of mankind. This leads to humility accompanied with the inevitable reliance on the strength and understanding of God the provider of life. On another front, a human considers himself worthy of sharing life with God and of receiving God's grace and blessing despite being weakened and crushed by his sins. Therefore, complete humility occurs when a monk places his weakness in the power of God. Basically, humility is: weakness in strength. So when I become worthless to myself, powerless and non-existent, I qualify to be present in the realm of the power of God and His presence. "For when I am weak, then I am strong" (2 Corinthians 12:10), "For My strength is made perfect in weakness" (2 Corinthians 12:9). Therefore, if a monk does not unite his weakness to the power of God or God's power to his weakness, he will eventually reach ill-conceived humility, which is belittling. On another front, if a monk forgets his weakness, he will fall into the danger of pride.

Humility stems from Godly love. If it was not for the union that occurred between the power of God and human weakness, which was manifested in Christ, humanity would have never known true humility. As such, true humility is the interchangeable Godly love between our perfect God and the weak human, between Christ in His power and holiness and the weak sinner. We can then learn that the power of God's love only works in humility. Regardless of how much a monk achieves, he still receives from God what is not his and what he does not deserve. This leads us to the question: Is spiritual growth possible in an atmosphere of pride and delusory praise? No!! Arrogance and delusory praise are evidence of a monk's sense of his own power and holiness and this erects a major barrier that prevents the monk from realizing his situation such that it is depleted of all protection and God's power abandons him.

How To Grow In Humility

If our approach to the life of worship of God is by complete humility, by feeling worthless, understanding that we are weak by nature, sinful and undeserving of God's goodness and grace, then our behavior towards others will reflect this humility, which penetrates our thoughts, minds, actions and all our dealings. Humility in the attitude towards others is the definitive sign of humility from within the heart in worship. A real monk is not angered when criticized, but wishes for more, because often but not always, it is the voice of truth.

The Principle Of Communal Life

To understand the truth about communal life, it must be mentioned that monastic life was never intended for repentance to be alone or about negativity when dealing with others. The purpose of repentance is for the monk to reach the living Christ and embrace his beloved heavenly groom who fills all entity, thoughts and actions. We cannot understand monastic life unless we concentrate on true love which completes the law of Moses in its entirety. This is the reasoning behind monasticism "By this all will know that you are My disciples, if you have love for one another" (John 13:35). It is then not surprising that the building blocks of monasticism is built on a foundation of love. Monastic life is meaningless without this solid foundation. One cannot be obedient, pure or become poor without love.

A loving person understands that he entered the monastery to grow in love. This view brings indescribable joy to a monk's heart. Sadness has no place in a loving monk's spirit. Anger and selfishness have no place in a loving monk's spirit. There is no place for harshness or criticism in a loving monk's heart. There is no avenue for arrogance or envy in the heart of a loving monk. Love is the key to a successful monastic life. Thus the lack of it is disastrous for anyone who claims success in his monastic life.

Love is "the bond of perfection" (Colossians 3:14), it is what ties two people together in tenderness that exceeds all tenderness. It is the bestowal of oneself "Greater love has no one than this, than to lay down one's life for his friends" (John 15:13). Therefore, love confirms monastic communal life that we live and affirm. Only love can submit but not enslave. It binds without imprisonment and obliges without captivating. Isolation from love is not right in the eyes of God regardless of a monk's deeds. Love fuses many into one body hence achieves a life of community.

Community Life: Its Reason And Purpose Is The Love Of God

Love becomes a virtue when its purpose is God Himself and resembles that which Jesus reserved for us "As the

Father loved Me, I also have loved you" (John 15:9). However it will not reach this level until it is naturally and spontaneously bestowed within us and refuses greed and self gain. God turns away from any love which does not have Him as its principle and sole purpose. All monastic works are brought to life with passionate love which feeds and nourishes it on one condition, and that it is, 'showing love for others by truly helping them, and not merely by talking about it' (1 John 3:18). If it was not for love that masks sin and fills hearts with the Holy Spirit, you would not find real monasticism.

Communal life in its essence seeks growth in the love of God. As such it is a life of exertion and sacrifice. Sacrificing one's self for another is the most glorious manifestation of love and the highest road towards it. With this understanding, we can define monastic life as a communal life where its members share and live as brothers. They are people brought together by the Holy Spirit and seek a common goal. Thus their life becomes a living expression of the life with God. In the scope of community life, the love which monks exchange does not come from a humanistic drive, but originates from Christ who is one with the Father through the works of the Holy Spirit. Therefore, a monk who does not possess love, is as far away as possible from a life in Christ, who wallows in a pointless life and follows the law verbatim.

Unity in love is a discipline that allows us to enjoy the uninterrupted presence of Christ, which He promised those who continued with His name "For where two or three are gathered together in My name, I am there in the midst of them" (Matthew 18:20). Communal monastic life sets the framework that is built from a living stone; the body and all its members, of whose centre is God where all the rays of love meet. What this means is that as much as we are close to God, so we shall be from each other and the closer we are to each other, the closer we will be to God. As such, monastic life becomes an experience of the love of Christ, which helps us grow strong spiritually.

The status of communal life is like the state of a normal being. Its members are healthy, each in their respective places, they move in harmony and are held together by the law, which protects the life in it. Thus it is a life that assists the monks in growing spiritually. Christ who lives in them and they in Him, supports them, in whose name they congregate with Him and with each other. From His humble heart they labour in the love of others and grow in perfection, wisdom, holiness, in the shadow and care of the Spirit of Truth with whom they stand.

The Practical Application Of Communal Life

Real communal life between monks in the monastery is a great witness for Christ. Christ truly lives within us, therefore, we must protect ourselves and grow by:

•   Communal prayer

- Community work

- Supporting one another, especially during difficult times

- Praying for one another, especially for those who are passing through difficult times waged against them by the devil

- Forgiveness of lapses and weakness that are part of our human nature

- Spiritual discussions that kindle the heart and pushes us forward

- Escaping anything that hinders each other's spiritual growth

- Having a simple eye that sees nothing but the best in others

Christ invited some of the faithful to live with Him in a special way, like monks, He unites them in a communal life. Therefore a monk accepts his fellow monks, because they are from God. Monastic communal life does not work by a monk selecting his fellow monks, which is contrary to marriage, where the couple select each other. A monk is invited, because he accepts from God his brothers who accompany him in his monastic life. A monk does not choose one monk over the other based on personal considerations, but rather desires to live in communal life with any other person.

As such, it is required of the monk to establish loving and understanding relationships with everyone around him without favouritism. A monk that avoids dealing with another monk has not yet understood the meaning of communal life.

We cannot ignore the fact that any human community is not free of disagreements and disputes and monastic communal life is not immune of that, because we are also human, and there is also the ambush of the devil. We are invited to congregate around the person of Christ until we settle these disputes, in brotherly reconciliation built on the love of Christ and not on personal feelings, that is the difference. Communal life brings hearts together through love to congregate around the greater love which is Christ. It is a life of joy and peace stemming from a single goal.

It is natural to have differences in personalities and ways of thinking in any community. We must persevere in creating an atmosphere of understanding and to bring each other closer. It is not important to grow our numbers and to spend many years together to create a monastic community. What is far more important is the essence for which we live together. Therefore our dealings must be sweetened with the spirit of the Gospel. This spirit is a fragrance that is smelt by anyone who is near or far and is comforted by it. This is the spirit which is described with humility, sacrifice and generosity. The only truth which brings together many monks in a communal life is not the name, the uniform or the place, but Christ who lives in each one of them. As such, it is our duty to discover Christ in every monk we meet with.

The Right Framework For Communal Life

In our relationship as monks, one must stop and ask: to where can I go from here? What is the right framework for communal life? We must take into account monastic behavioural guidelines. We sometimes place an aura of holiness on our heads, meaning, a monk can sometimes act as if he is infallible, his thoughts, actions and will are independent of everyone else, stubbornness in what we say and do. We sometimes act as if we are small gods, not requiring anyone or not requiring advise from anyone. Other times we look down on our fellow monks, while Christ humbly left His throne and became man and man saw Him face to face. In communal life, we are in need of this face to face encounter. This brotherly encounter is characterised by purity, clarity and humility.

Therefore, the right framework for communal life is encapsulated by:

• The finesse of brotherhood: Respecting each other and humility in treatment, without altercation and wasting effort in discovering what pleases others. Also, avoid disrupting others. Is my brother sleeping? I should not disturb him. Is he praying or reading? I should not waste his time. Is my brother upset or troubled? If I cannot comfort him, I should at least avoid troubling him! It is crucial for us to understand how to treat each other, how to build with complete love this community and how not to cross boundaries when dealing with each other.

•   Spiritual finesse: We often try to organise our monastic life, but if Christ is not the foundation, it is pointless. Our monastic life is a series of relations built on God. Disputes and altercations begin once a monk loses his spiritual sense in the monastery, because he loses God's spiritual fulfilment. Therefore it is important for everyone to revise his actions in light of the Gospel and what it commands of us. We must truly feel that Christ is among us in the monastery so that every one of us can breathe in Christ's fragrance. We can then pull each other higher and increase in enthusiasm and grow, feeling the responsibility of growing spiritually together.

•   Sense of community: Is for the monk to sacrifice personal interests for the benefit of the monastery. Sense of community is the deep feeling from within that this monastery belongs to me and I to it. It means that selfishness is removed from within me, it means I do not seek the realisation of personal desires. The monastery for us is not simply a place of residence, but it is holy ground, we do not slack or work forcibly in it.

These matters are presented to everyone's conscience and only a good monk is able to understand and implement. What is important is that we look deep down. A monk living in a communal life without a good framework is like an abandoned ground, a vine on a pathway and a city without a fortress. The real wisdom is for the monk to know how to grow his conscience and stick by it.

A Mirror Through Which We View Our True Selves

A monk's life is personal and private. A monk is the "hidden person of the heart" (1 Peter 3:4), meaning, he realises within that the kingdom of heaven is near, therefore he is invited to live a life of internal repentance. He knows his sins and his heart is in need of purification. All this does not conflict with communal life, communal life is not against private and internal life. In communal life, a monk delves deeper internally and grows from within, because in communal life he learns more about his weaknesses and negatives so that he may become aware of them and persevere against them. This will protect his heart from the dangers of isolation and loneliness. There is balance, which we must strike and that is, communal life must not be at the expense of personal life, and personal life must not shut out communal life.

Communal life helps us discover ourselves. There is a gap between where we are and where we need to be, where we think we are and where we really are. If we remain in isolation without facing reality, we become a product of our own imagination and begin to live a fantasy and become narcissistic. In communal life, as humans, we get to interact with reality on a daily basis. Interaction with others reveals the cavernous corners of the soul and what lurks in the internal darkness of the folds of the heart. From here we realise the wisdom of the great fathers who tasked the novice monk or a monasticism seeker with tasks that required the most interaction with other monks, visitors or the monastery's workers. This was until the Holy Spirit with the assistance of his father in confession revealed to him the internal caves where the old man remains hidden. This is to enable the monk to persevere spiritually and remain vigilant until victory is achieved over the old man. Therefore, it was no random act that God guided Saint Abba Pachomius to the communal way of life.

I once read a story about a nun who lived in Italy. She was said to have seen visions and her virtues were well known among people. When the bishop of the diocese to which her monastery belonged heard of her, he went to the monastery and asked for her. She arrived proud and filled with self confidence. He greeted her by raising his feet and asking her to take off his shoes and bring water to wash his feet. She was astonished and immediately became angry at the bishop for disrespecting her. The bishop then realised the truth, that she was fooled, living a fantasy of holiness and stature. On the contrary, Saint Simon of the pillar, when he climbed the pillar, his fellow monks reported this odd behaviour to the abbott. The abbot sent to him requesting that he come down and told the other monks that if he does not listen, then they should grab his legs and force him down but if he heeded and came down immediately, then let him be. When the monks informed Saint Simon of the abbot's orders, he came down immediately and they left him alone.

Communal life reveals to us our weaknesses and this is beneficial to us.

Group Prayer Strengthens Communal Life

Monastic life dawned in the early fourth century AD. Monasticism consisted of hermits who dwelt in isolation, who occasionally met especially on Sundays to receive the sacrament of the Eucharist. When they got together in koinonia (community) it was for prayer which was centred around monasticism even though it varied in its expression, psalms or Holy mass. Therefore, there is no separation between these two lives, the private monastic life and communal prayer. This deep symbolic isolation was an irrefutable reality in the long history of monasticism. No one was excused from circling the Holy Altar, even those who live in complete isolation. The reason behind this is that rooted in their conscience is the belief that prayer is one and cannot be divided, in that it is an individual effort in the cell distinguished by an intimate meeting with God, and as a group effort where the monks become one body brought together by the head, Christ. Whomever does not yearn to pray within the cell, will not yearn to pray with his brothers in the church.

Since monks in a community represent a small church, the church cannot exist without the Eucharist. This is an underlying theological fact with real life representation in monastic life. The importance of monasticism stems from the presence of Christ among us and within us, as such, monastic rules stress the importance of monks gathering around the altar. When a monk prepares himself to partake in the Holy Body and Holy Blood of Christ, he naturally reviews his thoughts and actions towards others. If he owed anything to anyone, he must try with all his power to resolve it, be it with an apology, reconciliation or forgiveness. From there we can reach deeper brotherly love, from which the monk's spirit is fused with others in the monastery, which dissolves isolation and deepens communal life.

Prayers of the mass or praises in the monastery are no ordinary gatherings. It is a deeply rooted unity which is authenticated day by day by the sacrifice of the Eucharist. The Eucharist is unified by the Holy Spirit that dwells among us. Communal prayer is in fact our meeting with God and with each other.

Isolation and love in communal life stem from everyone's involvement in the banquet of the One Body and One Blood and from everyone's involvement in the sacrifice of praise.

Discipleship In The Monastic Life

A monk's life is constant perseverance against the desires of the old man. Spiritual guidance in monasticism helps steer perseverance in the right path. On the other hand, it enlarges the spiritual life until it reaches the stature of Christ. The first pioneers of monasticism such as Abba Anthony, Abba Pachomius, Abba Macarius and others, understood a monk's need for a spiritual leader, because they understood the difficulty of monastic life. It is almost impossible for a monk to learn this life without the guidance of a spiritual teacher.

Monastic traditions strongly confirm the tie between a monk and a spiritual guide, who is also the confession father. Saint Macarius the Great said in one of his sermons: 'The disciples of the kingdom of heaven are in constant need of a guide, otherwise, their efforts will go to waste'. A famous example was recorded by Saint Bladeous who said: 'those without a guide are like tree leaves that quickly fall'. Saint John Cassian says: 'it is silly for a monk to think that it is not a necessity to have a teacher in his monastic perseverance'. As for Saint John El-Dargy who passionately wrote in "Sal-lamoh" (which translates literally to "to hand over") saying: 'we who wish to escape from Egypt from the face of Pharaoh, the devil, are in constant need of a Moses to intercede with God on our behalf, to lead us and to lift his hands for us till we cross. With his guidance we cross the sea of our sins and defeat Amalek, which are our earthly urges. For those who rely on themselves and fancy the idea that they do not need a guide are fooling themselves.'

The great fathers of monasticism explained the different stages of spiritual growth a monk experiences before he reaches the state of Hyschia, as in peacefulness, and the state of Apatheia, which is when a monk has complete control over his desires. Once a monk has reached this stage, he can then progress to Theoria, as in contemplation. One cannot reach these stages without a guide who has experienced and lived through these stages. Therefore, the purpose of spiritual guidance is to assist the monk in reaching these spiritual levels in a shorter time and with less risk. It is crucial for the monk to trust his spiritual father (who is considered an instrument in the hand of God) and to be trained by him, as he teaches him the features of monastic life and root in him the right understanding of perseverance and spiritual growth. There is a beautiful verse saying "Two are better than one...For if they fall, one will lift up his companion. But woe to him who is alone when he falls, for he has no one to help him up." (Ecclesiastes 4:9-10). The book of Proverbs echoes the same message by saying "The way of a fool is right in his own eyes, But he who heeds counsel is wise" (Proverbs 12:15). Paul the apostle clearly articulates this saying "Obey those who rule over you, and be submissive, for they watch out for your souls" (Hebrews 13:17).

There Is Need For A Guide Now More Than Ever

Fog surrounds everyone in their search for God, especially these days where foreign matters have entered the original monastic life. Principles and ideas have been mixed that it became difficult to differentiate between what is purely monastic from what has externally entered into it. Many red lines have been blurred. The mist has thickened and visibility has become poor. We are in danger of losing our goal, this is the truth and we must not fool ourselves.

The spiritual father's responsibilities are to restore the feet to the right path, to restore warmth to the heart, to pour oil on the wounds, to gently press on the swelling to relieve the pus of neglect and forgetfulness. There is an urgent need for a spiritual father who listens, cares, welcomes with open arms, prays for his children and sheds tears for them day and night, so they can be enlightened and finds joy in their successes.

It is most difficult for the soul to know its hidden desires. It is very good at fooling itself that when it finds out, it makes an excuse for itself.   The soul is like a mother that evaluates her child as beautiful regardless of how ugly they might be, and this is why the soul needs a guiding father. Like a mirror, he reveals to the soul its ugliness and warns it, then provides the required cure. It becomes clear why a monk must become an open book to his spiritual father, that he may read into it whenever he wishes. A monk must be obedient. As the level of obedience increases, the stronger his soul will be when he ages. His soul will remain young even in his seventies and eighties.

Through the spiritual father, a monk can avoid a lot of obstacles along the way. A monk puts his trust in his spiritual father to light the way for him, share responsibilities and decisions with him.   This requires a great deal of humility from the disciple and openness in discussions. It is not easy for anyone to reveal the secrets of their heart and their deep thoughts to someone else, only the humble can. The biggest temptation a monk passes through is the thought of: What could my father possibly say to me?!! I know everything!! I understand everything!! I know more about my situation!! I this, I that, etc, this shows pride and grace deserts those who are full of pride. As a result, this will cause, God forbid, falling or at least the dispersion or weakening of spiritual life. Monastic discipleship is a long road. It is joyful for those who experienced it truthfully and applied it explicitly and honestly.

The Actions Of A Spiritual Father Define His Characteristics

The first task for a spiritual guide is to draw out to the light all the snakes that have settled within a monk and crush their heads. He then holds the right hand of his son and walks him up the stairs of holiness and righteousness, step by step. It is clear that this is a difficult task and full of responsibilities. The desert fathers knew of the difficulties attached with spiritual guidance. They were also aware of the reality that the spiritual father will have to give an account in the presence of God for everyone of his children, who are considered children of Christ the King. Therefore, they completely refused to accept the role of spiritual fathers and considered themselves unable and undeserving of fulfilling this dangerous role. The monastic tradition tells us about some of the great fathers who secretly left their monasteries and lived in other monasteries without revealing their true identity and asked to be accepted as novice monks. Their motive was not only humility, but they realised the seriousness of this task. This was echoed by St. Basil the Great when he said: "He who has been made responsible for the rest must remember that he will have to give account for each one." If one of the brothers fell into sin, his spiritual father must warn him of God's judgement, if he does not heed and his spiritual father does not show him the path to repentance, that brother's blood will be asked of the spiritual father. We can see that the spiritual father's perseverance is doubled: To save himself and to assist others to save themselves. This strenuous effort requires the spiritual father to be gentle and patient, bearing his children's weaknesses. He must be kind and full of love to the extent that he is not just ready, but craves to wither away and to be vigilant for the good of his children. He does this not for the purpose of controlling them, but because he loves and cares for them.

A monk's life is full of dangers. Three enemies await him day and night and they are: the devil, the body and the world. There is no doubt that a monk needs an experienced spiritual father, one who has long experience in the desert and knows its secrets. A spiritual father must have vast practical experience in the art of spiritual war, he needs to be able to analyse the inner thoughts and actions of his disciple in light of the Holy Spirit and guide his disciple the way he sees is best. We can then say that a spiritual father is a person who is filled with the Holy Spirit, who has spent a long time in its revelations, and the Holy Spirit speaks through him. The most important gift from God to a spiritual father is differentiation, as in, the ability to read and analyse the situation and to provide the appropriate guidance. This gift, which clothes the spiritual father, inspires him to provide the right guidance and protects him from diverting with his teachings. The Holy Spirit teaches him how to hold his children so that they navigate through the wars that befall them.

It is also important for the spiritual father to be a living example of holiness and righteousness, a living icon of virtues in order for him to teach by example alongside his effective words. He leads his disciples by example in his speech, actions, humility, sincerity, etc. This in itself creates spiritual envy and motivates his disciple to persevere and stand fearless in the face of war and not surrender to his enemies. The spiritual father is the leader who walks ahead of the troops, when the troops see him, determination and victory befalls them.

The Desires Of The Disciple Determine His Duties

When you carefully read monastic tradition books, you notice that it clearly mentions that the first step a novice monk must perform is, to knock at the doors of the men of God and ask for their advice. St. Basil the Great made this law. The novice monk seeks a spiritual leader and sticks with him. The spiritual leader secures the monk's path and leads him in the path of righteousness with God. Monks used to embark on long journeys on foot, either on their own or as a group seeking one of the famous fathers who is known for his righteousness. Those brethren used to say to the father: "we quickly came to you, because we found in your life and your words many things that never crossed our minds." They submit themselves under his guidance with full confidence that this father possesses the words of life in his mouth.

After selecting a spiritual father, it is no longer up to the monk to interfere with his spiritual father's curriculum which he set out, even if it seemed strange at first. As long as the spiritual father's orders are not against the word of God, the novice monk must obey it till death and remain under his guidance for life, because it is forbidden to change fathers once they have been chosen. Novice monks are aware that their spiritual father love them like a mother's love towards her child. As such, the novice monk opens his heart to his father and completely submits himself in his hands. Monastic fathers warn the disciple against abusing their spiritual father's love, disobeying him or losing their respect.

If there were any words that describe the relationship between a disciple and his father they would be complete obedience. Obedience is one of the foundational pillars of monasticism. It does not eliminate freedom, but helps clear the mind and heart, which is real freedom. Obedience - because the monk trusts that the spiritual father declares the will of God and knows the true path that leads to peacefulness of the soul and purity of heart. Let no one think that because a monk lives in complete obedience that it means he has no personality, this thought is far from the truth. The desert fathers did not forget that humans are vastly different from one another; each person has their qualities and features.

The book of sayings, Apophthegmata, reflects the respect of monastic fathers to the diversity in the monastic way of life from one person to the other and to the diversity in personalities. As such, they did not seek to implement generic and strict rules for the novice as a whole. The Fathers appreciated and respected the different methods and gifts. They had faith that it is the One Spirit, who will work and distribute everyone's share as much as they required. Most Fathers agreed on the existence of personal differences and diversity in personalities from one person to the other.

As a monk's desire for the life of purity increases, so does his obedience to his spiritual father. In addition, his sensitivity towards reprimand from his spiritual father for his sins will gradually diminish. Reprimand, discipline and sometimes punishment are remedies used by the father for the benefit of the son, for the salvation of his soul and to bring him back to his senses. Therefore, it is necessary for the monk, through the motivation of the Holy Spirit, to submit to his father that he may realise and fulfil the will of God in his life. Let us look to the Bible's sayings, "How I have hated instruction, and my heart despised correction! I have not obeyed the voice of my teachers, nor inclined my ear to those who instructed me! I was on the verge of total ruin, in the midst of the assembly and congregation (Proverbs 5:12-14) and "A wise son heeds his father's instruction, but a scoffer does not listen to rebuke." (Proverbs 13:1).

Diversity In Teaching Methods

The laws of St. Pachomius clearly articulate the diverse methods used by the spiritual father with his children. It can range from reprimand, encouragement or sometimes punishment for the purpose of rehabilitation. A spiritual father does not continuously utilise a single method, but employs the most appropriate one for the situation. St. Pachomius says "the father must first give advice, then reprimand, and finally punishment". The punishment must be proportionate to the sin and the purpose of it is to rehabilitate. Rehabilitating a sinner, needs to be approached like a doctor would a patient. A doctor would not get angry at a patient, he perseveres against the illness not the patient.

In the writings of St. Gregory of Nyssa, he informs us that there is no essence to sin, but it is rather the absence of virtue. As such, planting and growing virtues is the best way to fight evil and sin. St John El-Dargy warns the spiritual father to take into account the son's personality, as well as his level, experience, age and preferences, and to always remind him of eternal life and the love of Christ in order to strengthen him in his perseverance for the sake of his salvation.

St Gregory of Nazianz (330 - 390 AD) explained that different people need to be given different guidance and teachings. Some benefit from simplified teachings while some need to be spurred and prodded. Some benefit from encouragement and others from reprimand. Regardless, the right method must be used at the right time and in the right circumstances to avoid negative effects. He goes on to explain that sometimes the father must be attentive to every detail while in other times he ignores it, meaning if he saw it, he pretends not to have and if he heard, he pretends not to have. This is tailored to the personality of the monk who is receiving guidance. This reveals the importance of a father who is wise and discerning.

St. John El-Dargy stresses that the spiritual father must be enlightened by the Holy Spirit in his teaching methods. For example, the spiritual father would not tell all his children that the monastic path is narrow and distressing. He would not say to every monk that the yoke is light, but he delivers his teaching to everyone according to their situation, based on their personality, nature, gifts, weaknesses, preferences, etc. As such, discipleship for the spiritual father is not an easy routine, but requires hard work, vigilance and special help from God.

According to our fore fathers' texts, there are two essential principals to be observed in spiritual guidance and they are progressive spiritual growth and communication. The principal of spiritual growth avoids extremism and miscalculated and temperamental leaps. As for the principal of communication, it is so that the father thinks with the son and not for the son. This requires an established and intimate relationship between the father and his disciple, trust by the son and love from the father.

In spiritual guidance, it is vital for the father to be clear and descriptive in his teachings so that the son can easily understand his teachings without confusion. The fathers words must be targeted and concise, and does not carry more than one meaning.

Conclusion

Leading by example is the best non-verbal method used for spiritual guidance in monasticism. It provides a higher degree of trustworthiness and is considered a seal on every teaching given.

The Three Basics Of Monasticism

Monastic life is a visible sign of the sovereignty of God. It is a symbol of the indiscriminate love which the world has never seen before. It is true that there are saints everywhere, however God yearns to find people who live in faith and seek everlasting life in a holistic manner. In the monastery, there are people who have left everything by their own free will and with a personal motive. Their actions form a crown for Christian life and complete it. It is a clear sign of victory. This is not because of the works of a monk, but it is God who finds the seed in them and uses them as shining symbols for the whole world.

These monks leave the old life for the love of Christ and to live a life according to Christ. God is everything for them. He is their love, life and possession. In this life, they discover things difficult to see in the world. They discover God's deep secret. The Monk is one who deprives himself of everything even of life itself so that he can continuously sit at the feet of Christ, contemplating, drinking from His words, pleased by His company and wandering in His love. The monk forgets everything, he no longer thinks about hunger or thirst, clothing, life or death. There is no spiritual meaning to monasticism other than complete adherence to Christ as the path of life and truth. We live in and through Christ and only because of Him.

If a monk lived the true monastic life, Christ will grow within him. Christ grows within us through our life and lives within us through our life - if we give it to Him. If we choose to give our attention to something else, how will Christ appear in us? How will we understand His will for us? Therefore, a monk must commit to the path in complete honesty and discipline. It is like the commitment to a contract signed with honour, signed with blood - the blood of the sacrifice he chose to offer on his own free will.

Monasticism is a special way of meeting with God. It has a sense of decree about it. God never ceases to be honest, His judgment never fails or changes and as a monk, I enter into an agreement with Him. I can either match God's honesty or do not enter into the agreement to begin with. This is what the bible teaches us "Better not to vow than to vow and not pay" (Ecclesiastes 5:5). As such, monastic life is about disciplining the whole life to live honestly with God. When a monk begins his monastic life, he must be completely honest in his obedience, purity, poverty. As the days become repetitive honesty can sometimes begin to waver.

A true monk is able to say to Christ: 'I no longer own anything, everything that is mine is now Yours for the rest of my life even my life itself'. It is a complete and unrestricted offering of the will, freedom and of one's self. This offering is to be without constraints that hinder the growth and the rise of the Kingdom of God within us. We must rid ourselves of anything that disturbs this Kingdom and this is the perseverance of the monk. As for God, He slowly fills the monk so that the monk feels that he does not require anything. God feeds the monk and quenches his thirst and fills his spirit until it overflows. God whispers to the monk: "Everything that is Mine is yours". This is the richness that the saints achieve in monastic life. They become deprived of deprivation, hunger and privation. God filled them and rewarded them for their offering with an abundant Godly offering. As much as the monk can be generous in his offering to God, so will God be in filling his bosom with Godly blessings.

Background Of The Monastic Basics

Christ our Lord during His life chose to live in a certain way. He chose to live in poverty, chastity and obedience. Likewise the monk chooses to live the same way Christ did, or more importantly, he chooses Christ the poor, the virgin and the obedient. In other words, the monk does not choose poverty, but Christ the poor, not virginity, but Christ the virgin, not obedience, but Christ the obedient. The choice a monk makes is for the person of Christ, as such, whatever life Christ Has lived and for whatever reason He lived it, the monk follows Christ in poverty, chastity and obedience.

The acceptance of a monk to Christ's call and the participation in Christ's way of life is an accomplishment and an expression of a monk's complete submission of his life to Christ. He adopts a life of poverty, chastity and obedience. The grace of the Holy Spirit accompanies him throughout his monastic life, and because our Lord Christ himself lived this life and said to the Father "for their sakes, I sanctify Myself" (John 17:19). Through His love, He called those chosen by the Father to follow Him and participate in His way of life.

These basics of monasticism are not some external mandate or an external show that is empty from the inside. On the contrary, it has depth - the essence of which is changing a monk's life from within to be present in God and to head towards Him. It carries the power of a new life; a monk no longer lives the old life, but walks the new.

If the purpose of these basics is unity with God, then this represents the sacrament of marriage in which one offers himself. When God created man, He was thirsty for the moment when He would unite with love with His creation - the unity which Adam refused. For this reason, God chose for Himself a nation, the people of Israel as a bride "As the bridegroom rejoices over the bride, so shall your God rejoice over you" (Isaiah 62:5). Even Israel was not faithful to the end. Thus every unification with God is to become a sacrament of love between God and the soul, a real marriage. The soul offers itself to God to be His and only His.

A monk chooses obedience, poverty and chastity as a life long promise in the sacrament of a spiritual marriage between his soul and God. The promise alone is not sufficient, but requires honesty in its application. The monk, in all honesty, promises to be for God. The monk lives this marriage as a life of internal joy and endless patience. Patience is a sign of honesty, because the monk is no longer for himself, but for another. In exchange for his patience, he is given eternal life "Be faithful until death, and I will give you the crown of life" (Revelations 2:10).

Who can keep these basics?

- Only the free is capable of adopting obedience.

- Only the mature is capable of committing to chastity.

- Only the ascetic is capable of living in poverty.

If a monk honestly followed these basics, it will assist him in becoming a vessel of absolute love for God. The absolute love for God soothes the heart and kindles unspeakable joy in the monk.

The Relationship Between Human Beings

If we focused our attention to the three basics of monasticism, we will find that it relates, in its essence, to three human tendencies which are core to human nature. These are:

- The relationship between humans and the materialistic world, from which the monk adopts poverty.

- Relationships amongst humans, from which the monk adopts a life of chastity.

- The relationship between humans and society,

from which the monk adopts a life of obedience.

These three tendencies are rooted in humans and they:

- Can lead to good or evil.

- Can be used for good or they can be abused.

- Can be used to reach life's ultimate goal (God) or steer away from it.

For these reasons:

- Christ is chosen over them or they over the person of Christ.

- They can remain as a means or become the ultimate goal in one's life.

- One can be free from them for the sake of earning Christ or become enslaved to them.

These three humanistic tendencies are filled with signs of good and evil together, which we will explain below.

The Relationship Between Humans: In The Materialistic World

God created man in the most magnificent image and made everything on earth available to him in abundance. God gave him power over it and instructed him to make use of it, for it was in itself good. However, sin entered the world right through to the core of humanity and desecrated the relationship. Humanity became divided between the will of God (maintaining a good relationship with earth) and the persistence of the evil to misuse it. And so, man became divided between: the use of creation as a means to reach the ultimate goal (God) and creation as a goal that not just obstructs, but steers away from God. This is why a monk chooses a life of poverty to free himself of his relationship with the materialistic world that he may become free to rid himself of materialism, which has been rooted in him. He is then able to prefer the love of God over the wreckage of this world. The internal freedom from the world opens the heart so that he can love God with an undivided heart. As such; the materialistic world becomes a means, while the love of God is the goal.

Relationship With Others

God created humans, male and female, in a mutual loving relationship. He created them in His image, and that was good. However, sin vandalised this beautiful image and love has since been misused. The human heart became divided between: its original use in the image of God and its desecrated and misused sexual form. And so, a monk chooses a life of chastity to free himself of his relationships with others, to become free of the other sex. Once he is free of the affection and sexual tendencies engraved in him, for he does not have anyone, he is then able to prefer the love of Christ over others and to love humans wholly, for his internal freedom from others opens his heart so that he is able to love humanity through his love for God and with an undivided heart.

Relationship With Society

God created man as a free being, free in his personal actions and his relations with other humans, and that was all good. However, sin made man self-centred and God was no longer the focus of his life. Sin had caused man to dictate other people's lives rather than having loving and respectful relationships. In turn, the human will became divided between: freedom for the good of others and freedom for the benefit of one's self at the expense of others. Faced with the tendency of autonomy and domination over others, a monk chooses obedience to free his relations with all humans. He is then freed from focusing on himself and is able to love

God, obey Him and submit to Him his life to control it. This of course includes the submission of his obedience to his spiritual father in the scope of his obedience to God. Therefore, the internal freedom from human society opens his heart so that he can love God through his obedience to Him and to others with an undivided heart.

These three humanistic tendencies are rooted in the core of human nature. They are good tendencies in themselves because God created man with a good relationship with them, however, man misused them as we have previously stated. And so, people became vulnerable to deflection from their relationship with God and their fellow humans. These are tendencies with an element of good, but man converted it to an element of evil. This double standard steers away without preference from the love of God and other people. This has made the monk choose what is above these three tendencies poverty, chastity and obedience that he may return to its origin, the way God intended it to be. In other words, a monk seeks throughout his life to deviate from what characterises his relationship with the materialistic world, other humans and society, by riding himself of assets, sexual affection and autonomy to return to its original and good form. This deviation (or freedom) is deprivation for the sake of expanding, but in a good and holy way, aggregating everything in the love of Christ.

The three basics of monasticism help the monk in freeing himself of all selfish tendencies. Freedom means, not being self centred, rather accepting deprivation for the sake of making the person of Christ the centre. This deprivation is death for the sake of life. It is loss for the sake of gain. This is what we understand from St. Paul the apostle's saying "But what things were gain to me, these I have counted loss for Christ. Yet indeed I also count all things loss for the excellence of the knowledge of Christ Jesus my Lord, for whom I have suffered the loss of all things, and count them as rubbish, that I may gain Christ" (Philippians 3:7-8).

Conclusion

If a monk treaded in monastic life in all honesty and seriousness, through poverty, chastity and obedience, he will achieve victories for the good of the soul and will experience deep happiness rarely experienced by someone living in the world. Only then can we get a sense of the beauty of monastic life.

The Principle Of Chastity

Love is a strong feeling that one experiences towards another. It is the urge to form a strong bond with them through a mutual relationship that develops into offering without expectations. God in His wisdom, created the human being with strong feelings for others. As such, humans want to enjoy that love for others. This is one of the wonderful works of the Creator.

The mind and reasoning say:

- Human love is a great gift, why waste it?!

- Sexual urges are too strong to resist.

- To share life with another is better than being single!

- Being with another of the opposite sex completes me.

While these thoughts may seem logical to the mind, they are incorrect at the spiritual level. Christ our Lord declared chastity in the bible. Looking at the matter through the light of faith changes the perspective of the human mind. Faith's reasoning is stronger and above that of the mind. Whoever understood the sweetness of God's love, happily adopted monastic life and chose chastity as an expression of this love. Since my Lord Jesus offered Himself to me, I will exchange the love by offering myself completely (body, spirit and soul) to Him.

Once God's love has taken over someone, it becomes easy for that person to let go of every other love. This explains why a monk who is going through a period of weakness and lack of God's love, would start to find matters difficult and begin to steal back what he once willingly left behind. Is there better enjoyment than that of the love of the created to his creator who loves him?!

True light, happiness and the most magnificent beauty will always be in the Creator. Can God's love replace the love for the other sex? Yes! The complete replaces the incomplete and the magnificent replaces the inferior.

In monasticism, we find that love between Christ (the groom) and the soul (the bride) is superior to and overshadows the love for the other sex. It is a direct love through which the almighty God that seems far becomes near and intimate. Marriage is a holy matrimony in which a human reaches God in the company of another. A monk chooses God directly, as in, he bypasses the means and heads directly towards the goal. The sacrament of marriage is pure, holy and magnificent, however, chastity is superior and even more complete.

The only, but strong, justification for choosing a life of chastity is entering into a spiritual marriage. This is stronger than the bond between the bride and the groom in the sacrament of marriage. This is what the fathers called, 'the deep love'. The love of a monk to God is personal and ultimate to the extent that he dispenses the love for the other sex. It is a love so personal and intimate without equal. Chastity is the status of someone who chose God to be the one in his life and it is a gift from God to some and not for everyone. God did not ask every Christian to follow this way of life, but only some, and they are very few.

As the monk continues to honestly live a life of chastity, the stronger the relationship of love will be and the easier and quicker it will be for him to cross the path to the Kingdom of Heaven and be able to experience heaven on earth "For in the resurrection they neither marry nor are given in marriage, but are like angels of God in heaven." (Matthew 22:30). Happy is the monk who has discovered the Lord in his life and does not turn his back on Him. Whoever searched for God all his life and sacrifices his life for Him, will truly find it.

Is Chastity The Reluctance To Marry?

Chastity is not as some would think, an unordinary state due to reluctance to marry. Chastity is the collective work of all the power of the body, spirit and soul to synchronise and work in harmony for a life of holiness and purity. Therefore, it brings together and returns the united human nature once again through the love for God. It is a state of complete inner purity for the body, spirit and soul - it keeps the human being pure.

Chastity, therefore, does not contradict marriage nor does marriage chastity. Everyone is invited to a life of purity, but the monk accomplishes marriage in its most honourable and superior state at the spiritual level where Christ, the groom, unites with the soul, the bride. The idea of unity with God through marriage has its references in the bible. We find it in the book of Hosea, Jeremiah, Ezekiel, Isaiah and the The Song of Solomon.

Some people disagree and say 'if we all became chaste, would not humanity become extinct'?! This is not a realistic assumption, because as Christ our Lord said, this is not for everyone. St. Augustine answered a similar question by saying: 'Assuming everyone took the path of chastity, it would not be evil, even if we became extinct, for if chastity and purity increased among people for the sake of love for God, it is humanity's goal. It is better to become extinct and achieve the goal than to perish by sin'.

Is Chastity Deprivation?

A monk's undivided heart, will, love and freedom for Christ have given him true satisfaction that he does not feel at all deprived. All the energy of his body, mind, heart, will and all his being and freedom moves towards the person of Christ and His love. As such, there is no place in the monk's heart that is not occupied thus there is no place for the word "deprivation". Depleting the heart of affection towards someone is negative in chastity and whoever continues in this state will create a painful form of deprivation. The right way is for the monk to seek to fill the corners of his heart with deep spiritual life that reaches to the heights for the love for God. The saints were able to live a life of chastity without difficulty because of the lack of emptiness in their hearts. There was no need for anything other than God's love. This idea of deprivation never occurred to them, only those who live at the body's level use it as an excuse.

We can say then that chastity is not a form of suppression on the human and it is not a form of imaginary deprivation. It is not understood unless it is looked at through the love for God. A chaste monk does not despise the sexual urge or consider it a sin. On the contrary, he has a lot of respect for it. He protects himself not because of an ill conceived fear of sex, but in the name of love for God to whom he promised to offer himself completely. Every battle a monk passes through to maintain his chastity, is honouring this holy instinct which God has placed in the human being.

The Difference Between Chastity And Suppression

The adoption of a monk to chastity of the body, spirit and soul helps him overcome selfishness bit by bit and rids his being of the love of self indulgence. This paves the way for the emergence of deep love and increases the monk's bond with God, for whom he preserved and protected his chastity. Chastity that is built on the ill conceived fear of the sexual instinct is not real chastity and it defames it. There is a big difference between chastity and suppression: The one who suppresses it is tormented by sexual matters. He cannot and will not admit it, because the poster of "I" prevents him. It is then relayed to the darkness of the subconscious mind where it destroys the human being, because it is not monitored. Once a chance beckons, a destructive force is generated, capable of destroying a human being's balance. The situation of the suppressor is then dictated by the "I" and is dominated by antipathy as he attempts to escape reality.

As for the chaste, he does not try to ignore the battle. He transfers it from the darkness of the subconscious mind to the light of reality where he can deal with it in all consciousness and freedom. He does not face the battle with the power of "I", but with the monastic values and disciplines that he chose of his own free will. Therefore, it is a matter of openness and reality. It is a reality of God's presence freeing him from "I". As such, chastity goes hand in hand with self control and it is the adaptation of spiritual values. It is the conscious commitment to submit this instinct to a higher being. It is the source of power, life and freedom, not suppression.

Chastity makes the monk strong, open, as clear as water, as clear as the sound of a trumpet, gorgeous like the morning sun. Chastity fills monastic life with solidarity and balance. As the monk progresses spiritually, these matters will seem easier. He will experience the power and deep love that emerges from the victory over one's self. He also experiences the joy of a comforted conscious filled with peace. A chaste monk is always careful, because he knows his weakness, but you will find that his sight is always set towards God.

A chaste monk controls his instinct with a conscious mind. He frees his vital strengths and directs them towards God's love through continuous spiritual radiance. As for the suppressor, he grows a poisonous serpent in the darkness of his body and mind – it is ready to bite him if he lets it or the opportunity arises. True chastity can be understood as a an ideology of giving and sacrificing for God. The chaste enjoys spiritual balance and comfort in the midst of his perseverance, stemming from the harmony in his spiritual and physical being.

Chastity lifts the body higher. It lightens the heaviness till a time comes where the body says to the spirit "Arise, shine; For your light has come! And the glory of the Lord is risen upon you." (Isaiah 60:1).

How To Keep Perfect Chastity

First, we must be wary of separating chastity of the body from the chastity of the spirit and soul. Chastity is one and cannot be divided. Constant ascetic perseverance is required (with consultation of the confession father) to maintain chastity. This is expressed in fasting, vigilance, prostrations, prayer, spiritual readings, etc. A trained monk knows where the temptations will strike from. The thief of chastity knows his entrances and exits vigilantly, be it the eyes, ears, thoughts or food - it should not be a surprise. The monk stamps all entrances with the cross, tears of repentance and a strong will. He who has a pure thought will have a pure body too. He who has pure eyes will have a pure heart and he who has a pure will, will have pure actions too.

A life of chastity through perseverance against lust will find its true meaning. When we die from the world and its lust, we are separated from the current of death. He who separates from this current and achieves purity, Christ will live in him. We can then see the wisdom of the Coptic church in giving the monk a leather belt to place around his waist to stop the spirit (the top half) from falling down to the body (the bottom half). In other words, he died from the bottom half.

The monk who sets his sight on purity, will seek it with all his power without faltering or languor and will not let it go even if his limbs were amputated. He will remain pure even if he died without reaching its peak. A vigilant monk who perseveres to maintain his chastity will discover the devil of impurity from afar and will prepare for him and will bravely disgrace him in front of the confession father by beating shame. A vigilant monk is careful to quickly expose his actions to the light and does not hide in darkness.

A vigilant monk reminds himself:

- Why did he leave those who live for this world?

- Choosing what lasts not what perishes.

- The days and years fade away and leaves behind a debris of bodies.

- The bodies perish and become dust.

- There is no marriage between monastic life and an impure internal life.

- There is no chastity without strong love for God.

- To escaping from places that cause stumbling is a means of securing the spirit.

- To monitor the body and keep the senses in order.

- To have strong faith in God's grace which protects.

- Of the Patience and hope that does not disappoint.

- To continue to persevere even if he got injured.

One of the effective weapons in fighting thoughts of lust is to continuously remember the name of our Lord, who lived and experienced a chaste life. Jesus lived this life to appoint those who resemble Him in chastity. The prayer of a heart filled with love and that longs for God, to be in union with Him, is able to convert all the energy stored in affection and the abundance of feelings of love towards God and the love God. If the spirit was truthful and honest in its love, it will receive the answer from God, affection for affection. The spirit will feel satisfied and become kindled as if lighten up with flame. It will find comfort and peace in God even if all its enemies are united against it. The waves of evil tendencies rush with force inside the senses of the spirit when ignited by the lusts that come to the body. There is no way to tackle it except by the power in the name of our Lord Jesus. The one who prays regularly will have a vigilant conscience, standing like a guard to control his thoughts and will not be burgled by the devil of lust who fools the inattentive.

Another important matter in maintaining chastity is for the monk to look with earnest passion to the power of the promises of God for eternal life with Him. This is where there is real comfort from all difficulties. This internal longing for the Kingdom of Heaven would make the monk in constant vigilance to be holy in body, spirit and soul, offering his body parts as a living sacrifice on the altar of love. The monk will train himself in living a holy life, which will continue with him in eternity. Meditating in the lives of our saintly fathers, who preceded us to heaven, will also give us enthusiasm.

It will become engraved in our hearts and lead for us our path being supported by their prayers and being delighted with them.

Reading the word of God, meditating in it and finding joy in reciting it has a major effect on irrational desires of the body. The work of the word of God within us is like salt that preserves food. It cleanses and purifies, protects and disciplines. It:

•   Disciplines the monk whenever he opens his mouth to speak in certain topics and not in others. It puts a barrier to protect him from speaking in trivial topics and from speaking inappropriate words.

•   Disciplines the tongue. It moves him to speak on the wisdom of God and His glory and disdain s him from speaking ignorance. It reaches the tongue in singing and the heart with melody.

•   Protects the eyes from desiring the beauty of the body to desire all that is heavenly. It grants honesty to the eyes and disregards devious looks.

•   Opens the ears to the speech of wisdom. It becomes a sensitive radar to the whispering of the Holy Spirit. It draws away from inappropriate conversations and the enjoyment of the fall of others.

•   Disciplines the hands hard work to reduce the energy of the body. It teaches them to be lifted for prayer.

• Keeps the thoughts pure – it does not think evil of anyone. It teaches how to captivate all thoughts for the obedience of Christ.

The Role Of The Spiritual Guide In The Perseverance For Chastity

How beautiful is this verse "Ask your father and he will show you, your elders, and they will tell to you" (Deuteronomy 32:7). "Two are better than one...but woe to him who is alone when he falls" (Ecclesiastes 4:9-10). Chaste life is both honourable and extraordinary. The devil has many colourful devious tricks to fight it. Therefore there is a need for someone who has been through these battles and came out victorious. The spiritual father can save his disciple a lot of grief because he has experienced the way to protect his chastity. It is then irrational to seek on our own, a solution for every weakness that could possibly affect the spirit, either by guessing or taking chances, while we can learn the ways form those with long and rich experience. Those with experience, through their experimentation, know the healing remedy. Monastic tradition has left for us a lot of sayings confirming the need for a spiritual guide in our perseverance for chastity:

• The elders who sailed through high clashing waves, now sail in safety towards the port of hope away from strong winds. They live for others who will follow their wonderful life. Like the tall light tower, they can safely steer us as well through the ocean of temptations.

•   Look to who has succeeded and passed through the journey with bravery and confidence, and sail with him in the breeze of the Holy Spirit.

•   Everyone who catches the scent of perfume that walked before him, will be perfumed with the pleasant fragrance of Christ Himself. Just like when a person lights a candle, from which all other candles are light, so will holy life transfer from the person who has reached it to those who enter his circle.

The path of chastity is one and has no deviation to the left or right. If we veered to the left, we will fall in sin and decay, and if we veered to the right, we will fall into extremism and defiance. This highlights the famous saying: "Whoever is defiant with knowledge, falls in blasphemy and whoever is defiant with asceticism falls in adultery". To explain this we say: For example, there is a monk who is battling the urges of his sensory, but he lives in false praise.   Such a monk is like a slave who wishes to be free, but instead of leaving slavery, he only tries to change his masters who dictate to him. He thinks freedom is in that change. He still remains a slave, even if he thought the first master does not control him, because there is another master controlling him and succumbing him by force. When his bodily urges momentarily calm down, he starts living in arrogance and false praise and so, grace departs him and he falls in the worst and ugliest sins. Other monks, after long battles against bodily urges fall easily in a different extreme to the right, and become easy prey for psychiatric illnesses such as anger, nervousness, cruelty, etc. They roll over their pain and suffer without anyone realising what they are going through.

Not everyone who successfully fights to escape the control of a certain pleasure endeavors to find the virtue against it!! For instance, will a monk who is escaping from desires find pleasure in tottering the body? Meaning, he gets rid of a sin only to find another in its place, either from the extreme right or left, they are both the same. Whoever said that fighting desires meant burning out the body with an extreme degree of fasting and hard labour? These matters then are balanced only by the confession father. He is the one to take care of his son to ensure his safety and treat his weaknesses with a real balance to protect him from counter intuitive sins lurking on both sides of virtue. The confession father is the one who can differentiate between giving something in the right dose and excessiveness, which leads to destruction. The confession father is the sensitive scale that says: 'let us not suffocate the spirit by degrading the body, and let us not be excessive with asceticism without reason, so that the spirit does not fall ill and with it the body.'

The Principle Of Obedience

When we talk about obedience, a question immediately comes to mind, does not obedience contradict freedom? To answer this question we must first understand the meaning of freedom. Freedom is the practice of truth and the fulfillment of responsibilities at the same time. This is the foremost of God's gifts to man. True freedom is a distinguishable sign of God's image in a person. It is what establishes a person's honour, which exceeds all else. On it, a person's responsibilities are built and it forms the foundation of justice (right and wrong). Freedom is a gift from God and God's gifts are without regret. It was given to man so that he can seek his creator and freely choose to live with Him and consequently reach ultimate joy.

Unfortunately, some have confused freedom with autonomy and completely missed the difference between freedom and autonomy. Autonomy means liberation from external constraints, where as freedom is liberation from internal controls, the likes of which affect the human in a number of situations far exceeding external controls in intensity. There is no ultimate freedom or autonomy for a human, but a human is attached to his creator. The onus is on the human to submit to Him, submission of the creation to its creator. Ultimate freedom from all constraints and of any realm is God's alone. Therefore relative freedom, which is for humans, is surrounded by natural, Godly and humanistic barriers.

We read in the bible about "the glorious liberty of the children of God" (Romans 8:21), which means obedience to the Holy Spirit – a kind of obedience that makes us truly children of God. This freedom frees the human internally from enslavement to all forms of lust and desire. A human's kinship with God, his growth, and the rooting of freedom in him are exemplified by the human's closeness to his creator, the fulfillment of God's will and unity with Him. Christ Himself came to return to man the freedom he lost "if the Son makes you free, you shall be free indeed" (John 8:36). Therefore, freedom ("freedom of the children of God") is a real internal adaptation stemming from God, which comprises the human as a whole - body and spirit. It is now clear the mistake people make when they think that freedom means unleashing the human to do as he wants and desires. Therefore true freedom is an internal one.

Christ alone can free from within. The commandments of His Gospel are the perfect law, the law of freedom. No laws are capable of maintaining a human's honour and freedom like the Gospel of Christ. Therefore submission to the commandments in the Gospel is not a constraint; on the contrary, it is a guarantee of protection for a human's freedom in its most honourable meaning. The image of God in a human is the cornerstone upon which one's freedom and honour lean.

True obedience to God is the desire to change internally to conform to the will of God and as we have mentioned earlier, true freedom lies in internal freedom. We now see that the difference between obedience and subservience is as clear as the difference between a slave and a son. What distinguishes a son from a slave is that the son obeys his father and fulfils his will, not because his father's will is foreign (external), but he makes it like his own (internal). The son relies on the father as his source of life. A slave however is driven by fear and subservience. A slave fulfils the will of the head of the household externally and it does not affect him internally. Therefore a slave does not see the will of his master as the source of life or freedom, on the contrary, it is the source of his slavery "For you did not receive the spirit of bondage again to fear, but you received the

Spirit of adoption by whom we cry out, "Abba, Father."16
The Spirit Himself bears witness with our spirit that we
are children of God" (Romans 8:15-16).

On The Example Of Christ

True monks have learnt obedience from the source of
all treasures of wisdom and knowledge - our Lord Jesus
Christ who "humbled Himself and became obedient
to the point of death, even the death of the cross."
(Philippians 2:8). For "though He was a Son, yet He
learned obedience by the things which He suffered."
(Hebrews 5:8). This is not strange for someone who
came to wipe the first disobedience of Adam with His
obedience. Since the first disobedience of Adam caused
death for all his descendants (because he sought external
freedom and autonomy from God), Christ's obedience
caused salvation (freedom from internal slavery) and
eternal life for all. The great Abba Anthony and all his
disciples the monks who came after him never stopped
obeying His commandment "If you want to be perfect,
go, sell what you have... and come, follow me." Matthew
(19:21).

The essence of obedience is carrying out the will of God
and His commandments, otherwise rebellion will occur.
A monk enters this obedience and preservers in imitating
Christ (the obedient) in his life. Searching for God's will

in our life is the essence of monastic life and all of us in the monastery work together in this matter. A monk who believes that obedience is confided in obeying the abbot or his confession father for some other purpose, has not yet understood the essence of obedience and is not capable of reaching the depth of obedience – he continues to live in an empty whirlpool. A monk obeys, with an acceptance and a drive from the Holy Spirit, his spiritual father and the abbot in order to realise and fulfill God's will in his life. Thus only the free monk is capable of obedience. The obedience of someone who has not been freed from slavery of one's self, is a kind of subservience. Only the mature monk can obey. What could ever mean the obedience of a child or a dependant?! Whoever has not reached a level of spiritual maturity cannot enter the realm of obedience because obedience requires an open personality and the ability to consciously undertake tasks and responsibilities. As such, it is the most honourable gift of monastic discipline. The spiritually weak is not capable of obedience, because, obedience is a monastic doing and cannot be fulfilled with a humanistic mind or by abandoning a deep spiritual life.

Monastic Obedience Is Internal Freedom

Monasticism makes available freedom strengthened by obedience, which frees even more from earthly matters and helps us free the spirit of slavery to one's self. This in turn, purifies the heart. Some accuse monastic obedience of diminishing a monk's honour. On the contrary, it leads to maturity by the growing of the freedom adopted by being God's children within the monk. Whoever follows Christ, the example of perfection, in complete obedience, will himself become perfect. And where there is perfection, there is freedom. As long as we live united with Christ we will be free, for the path to freedom is following Christ for life. Obedience grows this freedom deeper and gives the monk greater grasp over the direction of his life.

Since freedom is the ability to make real and valid choices, it is then up to the monk who lives his freedom to the fullest, to choose to return to the image in which God created him. This of which is his creator's invitation to him, through the removal of his nature and directing it towards the greater good. Therefore a monk can be defined as the free creature, who can, through grace, enter into a relationship of love and unity with God through his internal control over all that hinders this love and unity. Unity with God is the greater good, which is priceless, and with it, the monk finds the right freedom.

We see then that a monk's obedience to the monastery's abbot or to his confession or spiritual father assists him in reaching the greater good. Therefore it is obedience in Christ. The abbot or confession father stands by the monk and guides him to find God's will in his life to reach unity with Him. When a monk's obedience to them is through a clear heart and the fear of God, it always becomes a source of freedom.

The Correct Framework For Obedience

In order to identify the right framework for obedience, we must first affirm in our minds that the monk, through obedience, becomes closer to God through his freedom. He aligns his will with God's until it becomes his own. And so, the monk keeps himself constantly open to the voice of the Holy Spirit in complete obedience. The Holy Spirit works with the monk and through the monk in a number of different ways. One of which is to speak through the tongue of his spiritual father (who is already filled with the Holy Spirit), just for the very reason that the monk submitted himself in complete obedience to his father's spiritual guidance. Because of the son's honesty, the father gives the guidance and wisdom required for the monk to fulfill God's will. From here we understand that the right obedience trains the monk in responding internally to God's voice for it is fulfilled for the sake of Christ and through love for Christ.

We do not obey our confession father's guidance because it is in line with our thoughts and opinions, but because it guides us towards submitting our will to God. Therefore, obedience must be by comprehension and not robotic. Once I realise from within that obedience is beyond people, and the actions it carries out are for God, "Godly acts", I will then obey my confession father and abbot realising, and fully comprehending that what they ask of me is ultimately directed at revealing God's will in my life. It is not obedience without consciousness like military commands, but we obey God through others. We see that everything comes from God, so we obey. God looks at our internal state. We may obey for all sorts of reasons and destroy our bodies without gain.

It is true that obedience is not easy. We sometimes get annoyed for not responding to whom we obey or for disliking the work we have been allocated or for our lack of maturity. Obedience can sometimes seem dull, faint and unfruitful. The devil of sadness watches, he makes us obey without joy and steals from us the fruit of the blessings of obedience. Therefore the right way is to obey with joy. We spoke about this topic in detail in the chapter about discipleship in monasticism.

Obedience In The Lives Of The Fathers Of Monasticism

Monastic tradition tells us about the living examples of our saintly fathers who lived a life of obedience and reached high levels of spirituality, which we can observe in their actions and sayings about obedience. Saint John

Colobos (the short) is a great example of obedience. The story of him planting a dry branch and his commitment to watering it daily until it grew and bore fruit continues to baffle the Christian mind, but especially the monastic mind, by the sweetness of its obedience and blessings. Also Saint Paul the simple, everyone including Abba Anthony marveled at the simplicity and joy of his obedience even though he was an elderly. As for Saint Mark the disciple of Abba Silvanus, his teacher sent for him just as he began to write the letter "O". He dropped the pen before he could finish the letter and quickly took off with joy to meet his teacher, submitting to his teaching.

We cannot forget that Saint Benua quite often praised obedience and preferred an obedient monk over a monk who works. When they asked him why, he said: "The obedient puts the will of others ahead of his own, he suspends his desires and will to fulfill that of his teacher". Abba Anthony, the father of monks says: "Obedience and simplicity causes wild beasts to submit to us". Also an elderly father once said: "Whoever lives in the obedience of a spiritual father is braver and has less risk than the one on his own". Saint John El-Dargy also says: "Whoever is without a minder is not safe".

Great then is the obedience for the sake of God.